The
COCKTAIL
Directory

The
COCKTAIL
Directory

Kim Davies

CHARTWELL
BOOKS, INC.

First published in 2006 and reprinted in 2007 by

CHARTWELL BOOKS INC.

A division of BOOK SALES, INC.

114 Northfield Avenue

Edison, New Jersey 08837, USA.

ISBN-13: 978-0-7858-2017-8

ISBN-10: 0-7858-2017-5

This book was conceived, designed, and produced by

THE IVY PRESS LIMITED

The Old Candlemakers

Lewes, East Sussex, BN7 2NZ, UK.

Creative Director: PETER BRIDGEWATER

Publisher: SOPHIE COLLINS

Editorial Director: JASON HOOK

Senior Project Editor: HAZEL SONGHURST

Art Director: KARL SHANAHAN

Designer: GINNY ZEAL

Photography: AMP PHOTOGRAPHY

Illustrations: TONWEN JONES

Printed and bound in China

CONTENTS

INTRODUCTION

A good cocktail is a kind of liquid firework. It is a witty riot of color, an explosive surprise for the senses, a memorable and enjoyable treat.

There is an art to making cocktails and it takes some practice to get it right. But the difference between this and any other form of preparing food and drink is that with cocktails even your disasters are going to taste pretty good.

It wasn't always this way. Some of the first cocktails were invented as an expedient way to make rough spirits more palatable: fruit juice and club soda can cover a multitude of sins. These low-rent cocktails had their heyday during the Prohibition era of the 1920s, when drinks didn't have to be good, they just had to be available.

The true golden age of the cocktail was the 1930s, when a few creative bartenders and quick-thinking entrepreneurs invented many of the classic drinks we know today. Cocktails became rather chic, partly because they were still considered slightly risqué. Unruly talents such as Ernest Hemingway,

Scott Fitzgerald, and Dorothy Parker couldn't get enough of them.

The cocktail vogue lasted well into the 1950s, and there is now a renewed interest in these spectacular party drinks. Today the emphasis is on making them for yourself, according to your own tastes. The Martini is a great example of a true classic. It is a ritual, a lifestyle—and it's very in. But the new base is vodka, not gin, married with chocolate and fruit flavorings such as sour apple, watermelon, or cranberry. So have fun inventing your own cocktails—all the principles you need are here in this book—or you can customize these recipes by adding a little more lemon juice here, a mite less sugar there, or an extra glug of vodka wherever you like.

This book is arranged in tabbed sections. The first section gives you the basics of cocktail making—everything you need to know in order to make great cocktails, including what

A definition

"Cocktail is a stimulating liquor, composed of spirits of any kind, sugar, water, and bitters —it is vulgarly called bittered sling and is supposed to be an excellent electioneering potion."

The Balance, May 1806

equipment and which glasses are absolutely essential—and what you can do without. The book also provides information on how to stock your bar at home, and gives you the lowdown on some of the tricks of the trade.

The main part of the book consists of recipes. First there are twenty classic cocktails, along with variations that you can try, plus a little bit of the legend and history behind each one. The subsequent recipes are arranged according to their base ingredient. Spirit-based cocktails cover drinks based on gin, vodka, tequila, rum, whiskey, and brandy. Each spirit is introduced with a brief overview, and then there is a selection of delightful cocktails for you to make. Further tabbed sections focus on liqueur-based cocktails, champagne and wine cocktails (including fortified wines), and nonalcoholic mixtures.

An easy-to-use glossary at the back of the book covers all the essential cocktail ingredients you will ever need, plus there is some useful information on websites.

Happy mixing, and chin-chin!

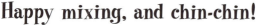

Setting up

The paraphernalia of mixology is part of the fun of cocktails. You don't need a huge amount of equipment but there are some essentials. Chief among them are a good-quality shaker and a selection of glasses: buy at least two of the main types of glass so that you can share the pleasure of any cocktails you make with friends and family. You will also need plenty of ice, and of course a decent stock of the basic spirits and mixers.

Tools of the trade

You will already have much of what you need to make cocktails in your kitchen. But it is also worth investing in a few specialist pieces.

First on the list is the **shaker**. This is used to mix all the ingredients together while chilling them almost to freezing point. The drink is then strained to remove the ice and fruit pulp.

There are two types of shaker: a regular shaker and a Boston shaker. The **regular shaker** consists of three pieces: a base, a strainer, and a lid. Having a removable strainer is useful: some cocktails are not strained, but are shaken with crushed ice and then poured straight into the glass.

The **Boston shaker** comprises two beakers, one glass and one stainless steel, which fit together. It is often the professional bartender's choice since it is larger than a regular shaker, but it requires a separate strainer, which fits over the steel beaker.

A **bar strainer**, also known as a Hawthorn strainer, is made from stainless steel and has an edging

Boston shaker

mixing glass

barspoon

strainer

bar strainer

of coiled wire to prevent spills. It is needed not only for a Boston shaker but also for any cocktails made in a **mixing glass**. This is a large glass with a lip for pouring; you could use the base of your shaker or a glass kitchen measuring cup instead.

You'll need a long-handled **barspoon** for stirring. This has a twisted handle and a flattish bowl, which is useful when you are creating layered cocktails (*see pages 172 and 173*).

If you don't already have one, you may want to invest in a **blender**—essential for Frozen Margaritas. You will need to crush any ice you are using

before adding it to the blender: an **ice crusher** would be the ideal piece of equipment, but you can also simply place the ice in a dish towel and bash it with a **rolling pin**. An **ice bucket** for storing your ice, plus **ice tongs** and a **scoop** for picking it up are handy, but not essential.

Measures

In this book, all liquid quantities are given in fluid ounces (expressed as ounces for short), which means it is possible for you to use a small kitchen measuring cup instead of a jigger. In the end, it does not matter whether you measure your ingredients in a cup, a jigger, or even the cap of a bottle. The main thing is to get the proportions between the constituents right.

A **lemon squeezer** is vital: you simply can't make a good cocktail using ready-made lemon or lime juice, and you won't get enough juice if you try to squeeze a lemon or lime in your hand. A **juicer**, though not essential, will allow you to prepare larger quantities of grapefruits, oranges, and pineapples, which will always taste better than the juices you buy.

Another good piece of specialist equipment is the **muddler**. It is a long stick with a bulbous end, rather like a pestle, which is used to crush sugar or fresh herbs before shaking or stirring. You can use the back of a spoon (a barspoon is particularly good) to do this if you haven't got a muddler, but it will take longer.

paring knife
zester
single-bladed zester
peeler

Good cocktails depend on getting the correct balance between ingredients. A **jigger**—or shot measure—will make you feel more professional when making cocktails. You'll need at least two—a half and a whole measure—or you can buy a double-ended jigger, which incorporates both. If possible, choose a jigger that has smaller measurements marked inside one of the cups. A set of **measuring spoons** is good for very small measurements (half a teaspoon and so on), but you can use an ordinary teaspoon and tablespoon.

Some kitchen basics that you'll need include a **bottle opener** and **corkscrew**, plus a **cutting board** and a **paring knife**, for preparing decorations. A **grater** for grating nutmeg and chocolate is useful. A **lemon zester** to remove the peel of citrus fruits will help you create pretty decorations, and a selection of **stirrers** and **straws** to serve with long drinks will add the finishing touches.

Other tools

Other equipment that you may find useful include pitters or a pitting spoon for pitting olives and cherries, corers for coring apples and pears, a large punch bowl, and a glass serving pitcher. You may wish to consider an electric juicer: this will make light work of juicing all kinds of fruits and vegetables, but it is not essential at first—you can always buy one later.

Glasses

Part of the appeal of cocktails lies in the way that they look, so it is important to serve them in clear, uncut glasses of the right size. Polish glasses with a soft cloth so that they are sparkling.

Many cocktails have their own glasses: the martini, the margarita, and the colada, to name just three. If you want to make cocktails, it is worth buying some special glasses, but you don't need the whole range. The most important are the martini glass, the Old-fashioned glass, the highball, and—if you want to make champagne cocktails— the champagne flute.

Martini glass

The classic cocktail glass, shaped like a capital Y, has the angular art-deco form of the 1930s. It is used for Martinis and for many other drinks served without ice.

Old-fashioned glass

This is a sturdy, straight-sided whiskey glass used for drinks served on the rocks—it is sometimes known as a rocks glass. It is also good for short drinks such as Sours and Manhattans.

Highball

This tall, straight-sided glass is larger than an old-fashioned glass. It is used for long drinks

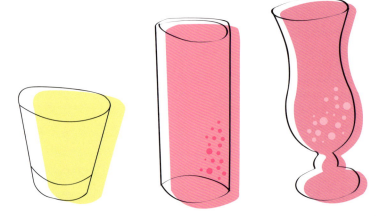

made with juices or sparkling mixers. A **Collins** glass is taller and narrower.

Margarita

Larger than a martini glass, this glass has a broad rim for holding salt. You can use it for Daiquiris and other fruit drinks.

Shot glass

This is a small glass that holds a single shot. It is used for neat spirits and for Tequila Slammers.

Brandy snifter

This glass has a wide bowl that narrows at the rim, concentrating the aromas of the brandy in the glass. The stem is short, so you can cup the bowl in your hand, which helps to warm the drink.

Champagne flute

The broad and shallow champagne saucer has given way to the flute. It is narrow to retain the fizz of Champagne, and has a long stem to keep your hands away from the cold drink.

Goblet

This is a kind of elongated wine glass with a short stem. It is good for large, fruity drinks such as the Piña Colada.

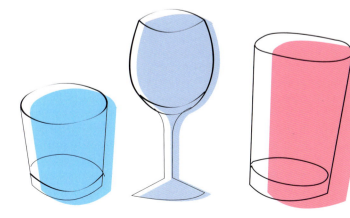

The essential bar

When stocking a home bar, be guided by your own preferences. Rather than buying a wide range of ingredients, it is best to begin by choosing a couple of favorite cocktails and getting everything you need to make them. As your repertoire increases, your drinks cabinet can expand accordingly.

Most cocktails are based on spirits, and a well-stocked bar would include a bottle each of gin, vodka, brandy, and tequila, plus Scotch and bourbon, and white and dark rum. Dry vermouth is essential for Martinis, and both dry and sweet vermouth feature in many other cocktails. Champagne, or a good sparkling white wine, is also well worth keeping in your home bar—nothing beats a Champagne Cocktail when it comes to celebrating.

Bitters add depth and flavor to cocktails. They are made from roots, herbs, and berries and act as a flavor-enhancer. The most used are Angostura bitters, but orange bitters are also worth buying— one can be substituted for the other in many recipes. Bitters contain alcohol, so do not add them to nonalcoholic cocktails.

The intense sweetness of liqueurs make them very useful cocktail ingredients. The range is

Did you know?

Vodka is classed as a "neutral" spirit, because it is colorless, odorless, and tasteless. This makes it easy to mix in cocktails. Many people believe that the basis of vodka is potatoes, but it is more likely to be made from grain, molasses, or wine.

huge—everything from Chambord (a French black raspberry liqueur) and Galliano (a vanilla and honey liqueur from Italy) to rich Kahlúa, (coffee-flavored Mexican liqueur). Among the most widely used are Cointreau, blue curaçao, Amaretto (almond liqueur), and Calvados or applejack (apple brandy).

The crème liqueurs also feature prominently in cocktails.

Despite their name, they do not contain any cream but have sufficient sugar to be thick and creamy in texture. Crème liqueurs are frequently listed under their French names: the most popular ones include crème de cacao (cocoa), cassis (black currant), mûre (blackberry), framboise (raspberry), fraise (strawberry), banane (banana), and white (colorless) and green crème de menthe (peppermint).

There are also ready made mixes for those occasions when you want to be spontaneous, among them Tom Collins, Bloody Mary, and Strawberry Daiquiri.

Mixers and other ingredients

Most cocktails contain nonalcoholic ingredients, which sweeten the drink and dilute the alcohol. Sparkling mixers include mineral water, club soda, ginger ale or ginger beer, tonic water, and lemonade. You will also need a good supply of lemons and limes, which are essential both for freshly squeezed juice and for decorations. Lime cordial is sometimes required for cocktails—such as the Gimlet— but don't use it when fresh lime juice is called for; it just isn't the same.

Fruit juices should ideally be freshly made at home, but you can buy good-quality fresh juices if you don't have a juicer. Where possible, choose juices made from whole fruit (not concentrate) and avoid those with added sugar. Some cocktails also call for fresh fruit purées, made in a blender.

Other ingredients you may need include canned coconut cream (for Piña Coladas and other exotic drinks), cream, milk, and fresh egg white. You can buy egg white powder from a specialist drinks supplier if you are worried about using raw egg—do not give a drink containing raw egg to an elderly person, pregnant woman, infant, convalescent, or anyone suffering from an illness, even if the drink is nonalcoholic and the raw egg is very fresh.

Making sugar syrup

You can buy sugar syrup (which is often called gomme syrup) but it is easy enough to make your own. Add equal quantities of sugar and water to a pan and slowly bring to a boil. Turn down the heat and simmer, until the mixture is shiny and translucent. Let cool, and then transfer the syrup to a clean airtight jar and store it in the refrigerator.

Spicy sauces such as Worcestershire and Tabasco are essential for Bloody Marys and a few other cocktails. You'll also need freshly ground black pepper, salt, and ideally celery salt as well.

Nonalcoholic sweeteners are often called for in a cocktail. Superfine sugar dissolves easily so is suitable for use in most cases, but sometimes a recipe calls for sugar syrup (*see box above*).

Other syrups that you are sure to need include grenadine (a red syrup made with pomegranate), and orgeat (an almond syrup) also features in various cocktails.

Ice

A good cocktail has to be cold, so you cannot do without plenty of ice. The ice must be clear: if your tap water makes cloudy ice cubes, then use bottled mineral water instead. Alternatively, you can buy your ice ready-made.

Ice comes in hard cubes, or cracked or crushed. When adding ice to a shaker or mixing glass, it is best to use whole ice cubes. They take longer to melt than cracked or crushed ice, and so they get the drink cold without diluting the ingredients. Crushed ice must be used in a blender; hard cubes will damage the motor. When adding ice to drinks, use whole or cracked ice, unless crushed ice is specified. Fill the glass no more than two-thirds full with ice.

Decorating

Nowadays, decorations for cocktails tend to be subtle and understated: one or two slices of fruit on the rim of the glass, a raspberry dropped into the drink, or a few cranberries speared on a toothpick. Serve long drinks with a stirrer—there are some pretty glass or metal ones available, or you can use a celery stalk or cinnamon stick in some cocktails.

Lemons and limes are the most usual decorations, in the form of whole or half slices, wedges, or twists of peel. Other citrus fruits can be used in the same way, while sprigs of fresh mint and slices of cucumber (*for Pimm's Cup on page 46*) add a pleasing touch of green.

Whole berries and maraschino cherries make good decorations, and you will need green olives (for Martinis), and cocktail onions (for a Gibson). All these can be speared on a toothpick or simply dropped in the glass. Whole nutmeg for grinding, semisweet chocolate for grating, and unsweetened cocoa powder for sprinkling—these can add the finishing touch to your drink.

The recipes in this book all contain simple suggestions for presenting your cocktails, but use your imagination, too. Just be sure your decoration matches the dominant flavor and color of the drink—as well as the size of the glass: a red fruit in a yellow drink will clash; a large decoration perched on the rim of a martini glass will look top-heavy.

Techniques

Chilling a glass

Always chill a cocktail glass, unless otherwise specified. The best way is to place it in the refrigerator for an hour or so. Alternatively, fill it with crushed ice and then tip it out before pouring in the cocktail. You can also place a glass in the freezer for 30 minutes or so to give it an attractive frosting.

Salting or sugaring a glass

Rub a wedge of lemon or lime over the rim of the glass, and then dip the rim in a saucer of finely crushed sea salt or superfine sugar.

Shaking and stirring

Fill the shaker about two-thirds full with fresh ice cubes. Add the liquid, and shake hard—holding onto both ends—for about 10–15 seconds, or 20 seconds if the drink contains sugar, cream, or egg. Strain the drink into the serving glass immediately. Empty the shaker, rinse, and use fresh ice each time.

When stirring a cocktail, fill a mixing glass with two-thirds fresh ice, then stir vigorously with a long-handled spoon for 10–20 seconds to thoroughly combine and chill all the ingredients. Strain into the serving glass immediately.

Muddling

Muddling is a way of mashing mint leaves, berries, or sugars before they are mixed into a drink. Put the ingredients into a sturdy serving glass, mixing glass, or the bottom of a shaker, rest the end of the muddler on top, and twist to break up roughly. Continue to twist the muddler, pressing down firmly, until completely mashed. If you haven't got a muddler, use the back of a barspoon or teaspoon.

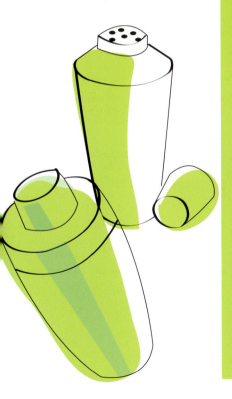

Shaken or stirred?

There is an ongoing debate about which cocktails need to be shaken, and which can be stirred. Some people say that a cocktail should be shaken if it contains fruit juice or sugar; others say that short cocktails should always be vigorously shaken in order to ensure all the ingredients are really cold. But often it comes down to pure showman-ship—making cocktails is fun, and shaking is a whole lot more theatrical than simply stirring the drink. There are also some practical consid-erations: never shake a sparkling drink, because this will flatten it. Also, if a cocktail contains egg or cream, it must be thoroughly shaken in order to amalgamate all the ingredients. Some cocktails—among them the Martini and the Negroni, for example—are traditionally stirred.

Floating

Some cocktails call for you to "float" one liquid on top of another: this works only if the liquid to be floated is lighter in density than the one in the glass. Hold a barspoon over the top of the drink, resting it against the edge of the glass with the back of the spoon pointing upward. Then slowly pour the liquid over the back of the spoon.

Making a twist

A twist of peel adds visual excitement to your drink. It takes a bit of practice to make a pleasingly regular helix—there is no shortcut—but it makes all the difference between a kitchen concoction and a professional cocktail. Take an unblemished citrus fruit (lemon, lime, or orange) and, using a single-bladed zester, cut round the peel in a spiraling motion (as if peeling an apple); then cut to the size you want. Try not to cut into the pith or the fruit—this is the hard part. Rolling the fruit on a cutting board before you cut can loosen the skin and so make the job a lot easier.

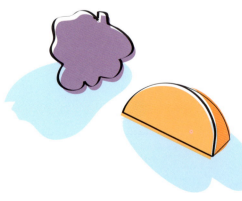

Classics

Thousands of cocktails have been created over the years, but very few have the indisputable status of a classic. These drinks are like little works of art: for some indefinable reason they stand out from the rest and appeal to every successive generation. Here are some fine concoctions, which every mixologist should have in his or her repertoire.

MARGARITA

Nobody knows the origin of the Margarita. The most likely story is that it was created by socialite Margaret Sames for a party in Acapulco in 1948—and that it is named after her. Wherever it came from, it quickly caught on, and remains a popular cocktail in the United States today.

••

Margarita
WEDGE OF LIME
SEA SALT
1½ oz TEQUILA
1 oz COINTREAU
½ oz FRESH LIME JUICE
TWIST OF LIME PEEL
Serve in: margarita or martini glass

Ᵽ Rub the lime wedge over the rim of a margarita glass.

Ᵽ Dip in a saucer of finely ground salt.

Ᵽ Fill a shaker with ice.

Ᵽ Pour in the tequila, Cointreau, and lime juice.

Ᵽ Shake.

Ᵽ Strain into the glass.

Ᵽ Decorate with the lime twist.

••

Blue Margarita
1½ oz TEQUILA
1 oz BLUE CURAÇAO
½ oz FRESH LIME JUICE
WEDGE OF LIME
SEA SALT
TWIST OF LIME PEEL
Serve in: margarita or martini glass

Ᵽ Salt a margarita glass as directed in the recipe above.

Ᵽ Fill a shaker with ice.

Ᵽ Pour in the tequila, blue curaçao, and lime juice.

Ᵽ Shake.

Ᵽ Strain into the glass.

Ᵽ Decorate with the lime twist.

For a **Frozen Margarita,** salt the rim of a glass as in the recipe left. Put a cup of crushed ice in a blender, add $1\frac{1}{2}$ oz tequila, 1 oz Cointreau, and $\frac{1}{2}$ oz lime juice. Blend well. Pour into the glass. Decorate with a lime twist.

Frozen Margarita

WHITE LADY

This classic cocktail is a perfect balance of sweet and sour, and its delightfully fresh citrus flavor disguises a powerful kick. It is served unadorned—as befits the elegant simplicity of the drink—and is drunk as an aperitif.

The White Lady has given rise to a host of sister-drinks, including the Green Lady (which is made with gin, lime juice, and Chartreuse), and My Fair Lady, a frothy pink concoction containing whisked egg white and strawberry liqueur. That pretty pink cocktail was invented in the 1950s at London's Savoy Hotel as a liquid tribute to Audrey Hepburn's performance in the movie of that name.

Chase the lady

The identity of the original "white lady" is a mystery, but the drink was invented at London's Ciro's Club in 1919 by Henry MacElhone. He was the founder of Harry's New York Bar, Paris, where he created the equally sublime Sidecar (*see page 40*).

White Lady
1 oz GIN
1 oz COINTREAU
1 oz FRESH LEMON JUICE
Serve in: martini glass

Y Fill a shaker with ice.

Y Add all the ingredients.

Y Shake.

Y Strain into a martini glass.

Perfect Lady

1 oz **GIN**
½ oz **PEACH BRANDY**
1 oz **LEMON JUICE**
1 TSP WHISKED EGG WHITE
SLICE OF PEACH
Serve in: martini glass

Y Fill a shaker with ice.

Y Pour in the gin, peach brandy, and lemon juice.

Y Add the egg white.

Y Shake.

Y Strain into a martini glass.

Y Decorate with the peach slice.

Bartender's tip
Make sure the egg is very fresh; it will whip better that way.

My Fair Lady

1 oz **GIN**
½ oz **ORANGE JUICE**
½ oz **LEMON JUICE**
¼ oz **CRÈME DE FRAISE**
½ **EGG WHITE**
TWIST OF ORANGE PEEL
Serve in: martini glass

Y Fill a shaker with ice.

Y Pour in the gin, juices, and crème de fraise.

Y Add the egg white.

Y Shake.

Y Strain into a martini glass.

Y Decorate with the orange twist.

DAIQUIRI

The Daiquiri has long been a byword for sophistication in America: Ernest Hemingway sipped them on his verandah in Cuba and later J.F. Kennedy, though no friend of Cuba, used to enjoy a Daiquiri before dinner.

The drink is named after the Cuban mining town where it was invented. In 1896, an American engineer, Jennings Cox, ran out of gin while entertaining. He added sugar to the local rum and lime, and offered the mix to his guests. A friend of his, Admiral Lucius Johnson, introduced the new drink to the Army and Navy Club in Washington DC.

Today's Daiquiris are a far cry from Cox's creation. They are often mixed with fruit and crushed ice to make a kind of alcoholic sorbet.

Daiquiri

2 oz WHITE RUM
¾ oz LIME JUICE
1 TSP SUPERFINE SUGAR
Serve in: martini glass

Ÿ Fill a shaker with ice.
Ÿ Add all the ingredients.
Ÿ Shake.
Ÿ Strain into a martini glass.

Bartender's tip
Grapefruit version:
replace lime juice with
1 oz grapefruit juice;
decorate with
grapefruit peel.

Frozen Strawberry Daiquiri

1 CUP CRUSHED ICE
4 FRESH STRAWBERRIES, HULLED
1 oz WHITE RUM
½ oz LIME JUICE
½ oz CRÈME DE FRAISE
1 TSP SUPERFINE SUGAR
Serve in: martini glass

Ÿ Put the crushed ice in a blender.
Ÿ Add all the ingredients except for one of the strawberries.
Ÿ Blend well.
Ÿ Pour into a martini glass (do not strain).
Ÿ Decorate with the whole strawberry.

For a **Frozen Daiquiri** you can add almost any fruit to the mix: banana, mango, raspberry, passion fruit—use 2 oz of your favorite, together with $\frac{1}{2}$ oz of matching fruit liqueur.

Frozen Strawberry Daiquiri

MOSCOW MULE

There aren't many classic vodka cocktails, since the Russian tipple was almost unknown in the United States in the 1930s. One of the first people to bring vodka to the United States was a businessman named John G. Martin. He marketed Smirnoff, but sales were so small that his business became known as "Martin's folly."

Then one night, he stopped by the Cock 'n Bull Pub in Hollywood. The owner made ginger beer as a sideline, and had a friend who was trying to sell a factory load of copper cups. In a flash of inspiration, these three capitalists combined forces and dreamed up the Moscow Mule—to be sold with its own copper cup. Martin claimed his drink had the kick of a mule. But it could have got its name from his stubborn persistence—which had paid off at last.

Moscow Mule

2 oz **VODKA**
¾ oz **LIME JUICE**
GINGER BEER OR ALE
2 SLICES OF LIME
Serve in: highball

Y Fill a highball with ice.

Y Pour in the vodka and lime juice.

Y Stir.

Y Top off with ginger beer or ale.

Y Stir again.

Y Add the lime slices to decorate.

Bartender's tip

While you can use ginger ale for these cocktails, real ginger beer will give the drink a wonderful peppery flavor.

Siberian Mule

2 oz VODKA
¾ oz LIME JUICE
2 DASHES OF ANGOSTURA BITTERS
GINGER BEER OR ALE
2 SLICES OF LIME
Serve in: highball

Ψ Put 2 or 3 ice cubes in a highball.

Ψ Pour in the vodka and lime juice.

Ψ Add the bitters and stir.

Ψ Top off with ginger beer or ale.

Ψ Stir again.

Ψ Add the lime slices to decorate.

Delft Donkey

2 oz GIN
¾ oz LIME JUICE
GINGER BEER OR ALE
2 SLICES OF LIME
Serve in: highball

Ψ Fill a highball with ice.

Ψ Pour in the gin and lime juice, and stir.

Ψ Top off with ginger beer or ale.

Ψ Stir again.

Ψ Add the lime slices to decorate.

CLASSIC CHAMPAGNE COCKTAIL

Some might say that to mix Champagne with anything is to gild the lily. And it is true that it would be wasteful, if not downright sinful, to make cocktails with a grand cru. Any *méthode champenoise* or even a good sparkling wine will do. The main thing is that you put the sugar lump in the glass first, then add the brandy, then the Champagne. The result is that the cocktail becomes sweeter as you drink it.

Classic Champagne Cocktail

1 WHITE SUGAR LUMP
DASH OF ANGOSTURA BITTERS
½ oz **BRANDY**
CHAMPAGNE
TWIST OF LEMON PEEL
Serve in: champagne flute

Ⴤ Put the sugar lump into a champagne flute.

Ⴤ Soak with the Angostura bitters.

Ⴤ Pour over the brandy.

Ⴤ Top off with the Champagne.

Ⴤ Drop in the lemon twist.

Southern Champagne Cocktail

1 oz SOUTHERN COMFORT
DASH OF ANGOSTURA BITTERS
CHAMPAGNE
TWIST OF ORANGE PEEL
Serve in: champagne flute

Ⴤ Pour the Southern Comfort into a champagne flute.

Ⴤ Add the bitters.

Ⴤ Top off with Champagne.

Ⴤ Drop in the orange twist.

To make an **Orange Champagne Cocktail,** put a sugar lump in the bottom of the glass, pour in a dash of orange bitters, then add $\frac{1}{2}$ oz brandy. Top off with Champagne. Drop in a twist of orange peel.

Classic Champagne Cocktail

OLD-FASHIONED

Like so many great cocktails, this fantastically mellow way of drinking whiskey came about almost by accident. In 1900 a customer at the Pendennis Club, in Louisville, Kentucky, asked the barman to give him a bourbon, but said he didn't want it neat. The Old-fashioned was the barman's improvised solution.

The drink became so popular that it gave its name to the short straight-sided glass in which it is served. It was also name-checked by Cole Porter in his song "Make it Another Old-fashioned, Please."

The perfect mix

You can use any type of whiskey for this, but bourbon is the traditional choice. The secret is in the timing: some say that you should take five minutes to mix an Old-fashioned—and much, much longer to drink it. Once the sugar has dissolved, the whiskey is added in stages, with one ice cube at a time. Stir very slowly so that the glass frosts up like a window in winter.

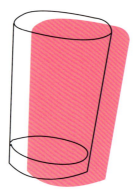

Old-fashioned

1 WHITE SUGAR LUMP
DASH OF ANGOSTURA BITTERS
1 TSP HOT WATER
2 oz BOURBON
TWIST OF LEMON PEEL
MARASCHINO CHERRY
Serve in: Old-fashioned glass

Ÿ Place the sugar lump in the bottom of an Old-fashioned glass.

Ÿ Drop the bitters onto the sugar lump.

Ÿ Add the water.

Ÿ Muddle or crush the sugar lump with the back of spoon until completely ground.

Ÿ Add the bourbon, together with 3 or 4 ice cubes.

Ÿ Stir slowly.

Ÿ Drop in the lemon twist and cherry.

Brandy Old-fashioned

1 SUGAR LUMP
DASH OF ANGOSTURA BITTERS
1 TSP HOT WATER
2 oz BRANDY
TWIST OF LEMON PEEL
Serve in: Old-fashioned glass

Ÿ Place the sugar lump in the bottom of an Old-fashioned glass.

Ÿ Soak with Angostura bitters, then the water.

Ÿ Crush until dissolved, using a muddler or the back of a spoon.

Ÿ Add 2 or 3 ice cubes.

Ÿ Pour in the brandy and stir.

Ÿ Drop the lemon twist into the drink.

SINGAPORE SLING

A barman at the Raffles Hotel in Singapore invented this drink as a variation on the Gin Sling (*see page 73*). Its sweet-sour taste and blush-pink color made a hit with English ladies who socialized there.

The days of the British Empire are gone, and the original recipe has been lost, but the Singapore Sling is still a popular drink. Some recipes include fruit juices to make it more refreshing, or a dash of grenadine to deepen the color; others omit the club soda to make it stronger.

Raffles Singapore Sling

1 oz GIN
½ oz CHERRY BRANDY
½ oz BENEDICTINE
½ oz COINTREAU
½ oz LIME JUICE
1 oz PINEAPPLE JUICE
1 oz ORANGE JUICE
DASH OF ANGOSTURA BITTERS
CLUB SODA
SLICE OF PINEAPPLE OR ORANGE
SLICE OF LEMON
MARASCHINO CHERRY
Serve in: highball

- Fill a shaker with ice.
- Pour in the gin, cherry brandy, Benedictine, Cointreau, and fruit juices.
- Add the bitters.
- Shake.
- Strain into a highball.
- Top off with club soda.
- Stir.
- Decorate with the fruit slices and the cherry.

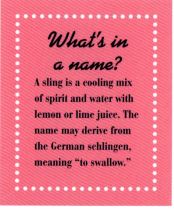

What's in a name?

A sling is a cooling mix of spirit and water with lemon or lime juice. The name may derive from the German schlingen, meaning "to swallow."

For a **Singapore Sling,**
fill a cocktail shaker with ice cubes.
Pour in 2 oz gin, and 1 oz each of cherry brandy,
orange curaçao, and lemon juice. Shake. Pour into
a highball filled with ice, top off with club soda,
and stir. Decorate with a lemon slice
and a maraschino or fresh cherry.

Singapore Sling

SIDECAR

This is one of several classic cocktails that was first mixed at Harry's New York Bar in Paris. It was invented during the First World War, and is said to have been named after the preferred mode of transport of an army captain who drank there. One day he is said to have asked bartender Harry MacElhone for an aperitif that would help a cold—the result was this mix of warming Cognac, cleansing lemon juice, and sweet Cointreau.

Two parts strong, one part sour, and one part sweet are the ideal proportions for this fine drink—though some people insist on equal measures. However you take your Sidecar, the glass should be ice-cold and it is essential to use good brandy and freshly squeezed lemon—this is no place to skimp on ingredients. You can dip the glass in lemon juice and coat the rim in crushed sugar if you like.

Sidecar

1½ oz **BRANDY**
¾ oz **COINTREAU**
¾ oz **LEMON JUICE**
TWIST OF LEMON PEEL
Serve in: martini glass

Ÿ Fill a shaker with ice.

Ÿ Add the brandy, Cointreau, and lemon juice.

Ÿ Shake.

Ÿ Strain into the glass.

Ÿ Decorate with the lemon twist.

Rum Sidecar

1½ oz GOLD RUM
¾ oz COINTREAU
¾ oz LEMON JUICE
TWIST OF LEMON PEEL
Serve in: martini glass, chilled

Y Fill a shaker with ice.

Y Pour in the rum, Cointreau, and lemon juice.

Y Shake, then strain into the chilled martini glass.

Y Decorate with the lemon twist.

Champagne Sidecar

1½ oz BRANDY
¾ oz COINTREAU
¾ oz LEMON JUICE
CHAMPAGNE
TWIST OF LEMON PEEL
Serve in: champagne flute, chilled

Y Fill a shaker with ice.

Y Add the brandy, Cointreau, and lemon juice.

Y Shake, then strain into the chilled champagne flute.

Y Top off with Champagne.

Y Decorate with the lemon twist.

TEQUILA SUNRISE

This modern classic is gloriously colorful, evoking exotic beaches and long, hot evenings. It had its heyday in the 1970s, when long fruit cocktails decorated with paper umbrellas were all the rage. It is still popular, possibly because it is so easy to mix and drink. It is often served with a straw so that you taste the grenadine first, then get the tequila hit.

Tequila Sunrise

2 oz TEQUILA
5 oz ORANGE JUICE
½ oz GRENADINE
SLICE OF LIME
Serve in: highball

> **Bartender's tip**
> Add the grenadine last.
> Add it very slowly,
> tilting the glass and
> pouring the grenadine
> down the side.

☿ Fill a shaker with ice.

☿ Pour in the tequila and orange juice.

☿ Shake, then strain into a highball filled with ice.

☿ Add the grenadine slowly, so that it sinks down to the bottom of the glass.

☿ Decorate with the lime slice.

Thai Sunrise

2 oz TEQUILA
1 oz COINTREAU
1 oz FRESH LIME JUICE
HALF A MANGO, DICED
DASH OF GRENADINE
1 CUP OF CRUSHED ICE
TWIST OF LIME PEEL
Serve in: goblet or margarita glass

☿ Place the tequila, Cointreau, lime juice, diced mango, and grenadine in a blender.

☿ Blend.

☿ Add the crushed ice.

☿ Blend again.

☿ Pour into a goblet or margarita glass.

☿ Decorate with the lime twist.

For a **Tequila Sunset,** fill a shaker with crushed ice. Pour in 1 oz tequila, 4 oz orange juice, and 1 oz lemon juice. Pour into a martini glass (do not strain). Slowly float in ½ oz crème de cassis over a spoon, and decorate with a lemon twist.

Tequila Sunrise

TOM COLLINS

The Tom Collins—made with gin, lemon juice, sugar, and club soda—has spawned a whole family of cocktails: among others you can enjoy a Rum Collins, a Vodka Collins, and a Tequila Collins.

The likely creator of the original drink was a 19th-century London pub landlord called John Collins. He used a sweetened gin dubbed "Old Tom." The name of the gin somehow became conflated with the name of the landlord, and so his drink came to be called a Tom Collins.

To add to the confusion, there is a separate drink called a John Collins that uses whiskey in place of the gin. Some people say that this drink emerged during the American Civil War, and that it is the grandaddy of the extensive Collins clan.

Whatever the truth, the Tom Collins is a fabulous thirst-quencher. It's traditionally served in a well-chilled long highball—also known as a Collins glass—and drunk through a straw.

....

Tom Collins

2 oz GIN
2 oz LEMON JUICE
1 TSP SUPERFINE SUGAR
CLUB SODA
SLICE OF LEMON
Serve in: highball

℧ Fill a shaker with ice cubes.

℧ Pour in the gin and lemon juice.

℧ Add the sugar.

℧ Shake well.

℧ Strain into a highball filled with ice.

℧ Top off with club soda.

℧ Stir.

℧ Decorate with the lemon slice.

John Collins

2 oz WHISKEY
2 oz LEMON JUICE
1 TSP SUPERFINE SUGAR
CLUB SODA
SLICE OF ORANGE
MARASCHINO CHERRY
Serve in: highball

- Fill a shaker with ice cubes.
- Add the whiskey, lemon juice, and sugar.
- Shake, then strain into a highball filled with ice.
- Top off with soda and stir.
- Add the orange slice and cherry to decorate.

Vodka Collins

2 oz VODKA
2 oz LEMON JUICE
1 TSP SUPERFINE SUGAR
CLUB SODA
SLICE OF LIME
Serve in: highball

- Fill a shaker with ice cubes.
- Pour in the vodka and lemon juice.
- Add the sugar, and shake well.
- Strain into a highball filled with ice.
- Add the club soda.
- Stir.
- Decorate with the lime slice.

Bartender's tip
Try using lime vodka for an extra twist.

PIMM'S CUP

The Pimm's Cup recipe remains a secret. It was invented in the 1820s by James Pimm for his customers at his London oyster bar. His homemade cup—a combination of fruit, herbs, and spices preserved in gin—became so popular that Pimm began to sell it by the bottle.

Pimm's Original

2 oz **PIMM'S NO 1 CUP**
½ oz **GIN**
LEMONADE
FEW MINT LEAVES
SLICES OF ORANGE AND LEMON
WEDGES OF APPLE
SLICES OF CUCUMBER
Serve in: highball

Bartender's tip
Gently bruise the mint leaves to help release their aroma and then drop them into the drink with the fruit slices.

Ⴁ Fill a highball with ice.

Ⴁ Pour in the Pimm's and gin.

Ⴁ Stir.

Ⴁ Top off with lemonade.

Ⴁ Stir again.

Ⴁ Decorate with the mint leaves, orange, lemon, apple, and cucumber.

Ginger Pimm's

2 oz **PIMM'S NO 1 CUP**
½ oz **GIN**
GINGER ALE
FEW MINT LEAVES
SLICES OF ORANGE AND LEMON
WEDGES OF APPLE
SLICES OF CUCUMBER
Serve in: highball

Ⴁ Pour the Pimm's and gin into a highball filled with ice.

Ⴁ Stir.

Ⴁ Top off with ginger ale, and stir again.

Ⴁ Decorate with the mint, orange, lemon, apple, and cucumber.

To make a **Vodka Pimm's,**
follow the recipe for the Pimm's Original,
but replace the Pimm's No 1 Cup with the same
quantity of Pimm's Vodka Cup, and replace the
gin with the same amount of vodka.
Decorate with mint leaves, apple slices,
and cucumber.

Vodka Pimm's

MINT JULEP

If Pimm's Cup brings to mind an English summer, then the Mint Julep is the flavor of the American South. This superb combination of mint and bourbon is the traditional beverage of the Kentucky Derby.

The Mint Julep is one of the oldest of all cocktails. It dates back to the 1700s and probably comes from Virginia. It was originally made with rum or rye whiskey, but is now always made with bourbon, which has a sweeter flavor.

Strictly speaking, the cocktail should be drunk from a silver julep cup, but you can serve it in a highball or Old-fashioned glass. Ideally the mint will be muddled in the glass to release the fresh aromas, but some people prefer it stirred for a more subtle flavor.

Mint Julep

1 TSP SUPERFINE SUGAR
8–10 MINT LEAVES, PLUS SPRIG TO DECORATE
2 TSP HOT WATER
2 oz BOURBON
Serve in: Old-fashioned glass

Ᵽ Put the sugar and mint leaves in an Old-fashioned glass with the water.

Ᵽ Muddle, or mash with the back of a teaspoon, until the sugar is dissolved.

Ᵽ Fill the glass with crushed ice.

Ᵽ Pour in the bourbon.

Ᵽ Stir lightly.

Ᵽ Decorate with the mint sprig.

What's in a name?

Julep is a French word derived from the Arabic julab, which means "sweet drink."

Frozen Julep

½ CUP CRUSHED ICE
2 oz BOURBON
1 oz LEMON JUICE
8–10 MINT LEAVES, PLUS SPRIG TO DECORATE
1 TBSP SUGAR SYRUP (SEE PAGE 19)
Serve in: Old-fashioned glass

Ⴤ Place the crushed ice, bourbon, lemon juice, and mint in a blender.

Ⴤ Add the sugar syrup.

Ⴤ Blend until well mixed.

Ⴤ Pour into an Old-fashioned glass (do not strain).

Ⴤ Decorate with the mint sprig.

Brandy Julep

5 MINT LEAVES, PLUS EXTRA SPRIG TO DECORATE
1 TSP SUGAR
2 TSP HOT WATER
2 oz BRANDY
Serve in: Old-fashioned glass

Ⴤ Put the mint leaves, sugar, and hot water into an Old-fashioned glass.

Ⴤ Muddle or crush until the sugar has dissolved.

Ⴤ Fill the glass with crushed ice.

Ⴤ Add the brandy.

Ⴤ Stir lightly.

Ⴤ Decorate with the mint sprig.

MAI TAI

The Mai Tai is one of those fruity long cocktails that conjure up exotic, palm-fringed beaches. It was a vogueish drink in the 1970s, when it would be decorated with as many tropical fruits as the bartender could cram onto a toothpick.

Classic Mai Tai

1 oz WHITE RUM
1 oz DARK RUM
½ oz ORANGE CURAÇAO
½ oz ORGEAT SYRUP
½ oz FRESH LIME JUICE
1 TBSP GRENADINE
WEDGE OF LIME
Serve in: highball

Bartender's tip
If you can't find Orgeat, you can use Amaretto instead.

- Fill a shaker with ice.
- Pour in the rums, curaçao, orgeat, lime juice, and grenadine.
- Shake.
- Strain into a highball, half-filled with crushed ice.
- Decorate with the lime wedge.

Fruity Mai Tai

1 oz WHITE RUM
1 oz DARK RUM
¾ oz COINTREAU
3 oz ORANGE JUICE
3 oz PINEAPPLE JUICE
1 oz GRENADINE
WEDGE OF PINEAPPLE
Serve in: highball

- Fill a shaker with ice.
- Add all the ingredients except the pineapple wedge.
- Shake.
- Strain into a highball half-filled with crushed ice.
- Decorate with the pineapple wedge speared onto a toothpick.

In 1944, Californian barman "Trader Vic" Bergeron invented the Mai Tai. Legend has it that the first people to drink it were a Tahitian couple who exclaimed "Mai Tai—Roe Ae," meaning "Out of this world!", and so the drink was named.

Classic Mai Tai

LONG ISLAND ICED TEA

There is no tea involved in this cocktail; instead cola is added to a strong spirit base, giving it the genteel appearance of an iced beverage. Originally, any spirit was used. But the modern recipe uses five: gin, vodka, tequila, rum, and Cointreau, which should be added in equal measures. There is plenty of scope for experimenting: try Alaskan Iced Tea (with blue curaçao instead of Cointreau).

What's the story?

Some say Long Island Iced Tea dates back to Prohibition, when sweet mixers were needed to mask the taste of illegal liquor. Another story is that bored housewives made up the combination in the 1950s, so that they could enjoy a drink while maintaining an air of respectability—hence the innocent-sounding name of this cocktail.

Long Island Iced Tea

½ oz **GIN**
½ oz **VODKA**
½ oz **TEQUILA**
½ oz **WHITE RUM**
½ oz **COINTREAU**
1 oz **LEMON JUICE**
DASH OF COLA
WEDGE OF LEMON
Serve in: highball

℥ Fill a shaker with ice.

℥ Add all the ingredients except the cola and lemon wedge.

℥ Shake.

℥ Strain into a highball filled with ice.

℥ Add the cola and stir.

℥ Decorate with the lemon wedge.

Long Beach Iced Tea

½ oz **GIN**
½ oz **VODKA**
½ oz **TEQUILA**
½ oz **WHITE RUM**
½ oz **COINTREAU**
1 oz **LEMON JUICE**
DASH OF CRANBERRY JUICE
WEDGE OF LEMON
Serve in: highball

℺ Add all the spirits and the lemon juice to a shaker filled with ice.

℺ Shake.

℺ Strain into a highball filled with ice.

℺ Add the cranberry juice and stir.

℺ Decorate with the lemon wedge.

Raspberry Long Island Iced Tea

½ oz **GIN**
½ oz **VODKA**
½ oz **TEQUILA**
½ oz **WHITE RUM**
½ oz **COINTREAU**
1 oz **LEMON JUICE**
½ oz **CRÈME DE FRAMBOISE**
WEDGE OF LEMON
Serve in: highball

℺ Fill a shaker with ice.

℺ Add all the ingredients except the lemon wedge.

℺ Shake.

℺ Strain into a highball filled with ice.

℺ Decorate with the lemon wedge.

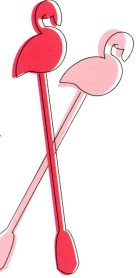

ZOMBIE

This lethal cocktail is a deceptively smooth and fruity blend that slips down too easily. It was created by bartender Don Beach in the 1930s who first mixed it at his Hollywood restaurant to help a customer over a hangover. On his next visit, the man was asked whether the cure had worked. When he replied that it had made him feel like a zombie, the cocktail had its name. There are many recipes for the Zombie, but the essential ingredients are rum, fruit juice, and plenty of ice. For an authentic Zombie, you need a dash of overproof rum floating on top.

Zombie

1 oz **WHITE RUM**
1 oz **GOLD RUM**
1 oz **DARK RUM**
1 oz **APRICOT BRANDY**
1 oz **PINEAPPLE JUICE**
1 oz **ORANGE JUICE**
½ oz **LIME JUICE**
DASH OF ORGEAT OR AMARETTO
½ oz **OVERPROOF RUM**
WEDGE OF PINEAPPLE
MARASCHINO CHERRY
Serve in: highball

Did you know?
Overproof rum refers to an aromatic dark rum that is highly potent; it shouldn't be drunk straight. It is also known as 151 rum, and the best-known brand is Bacardi 151.

Ÿ Fill a shaker with ice.
Ÿ Pour in the white, gold, and dark rums.
Ÿ Add the apricot brandy, juices, and orgeat or Amaretto.
Ÿ Shake.
Ÿ Strain into a highball filled with ice.
Ÿ Add the overproof rum, pouring it over the back of a spoon so that it floats on top.
Ÿ Decorate with the pineapple wedge and cherry.

Bitter Zombie

1 oz WHITE RUM
1 oz GOLD RUM
1 oz DARK RUM
1 oz ORANGE JUICE
1 oz GRAPEFRUIT JUICE
½ oz LEMON JUICE
DASH OF ANGOSTURA BITTERS
1 TSP BROWN SUGAR
TWIST OF ORANGE PEEL

Serve in: highball

Y Fill a shaker with ice.

Y Pour in the white, gold, and dark rums.

Y Add the juices.

Y Add the bitters and sugar.

Y Shake well.

Y Pour into a highball filled with ice.

Y Decorate with the orange twist.

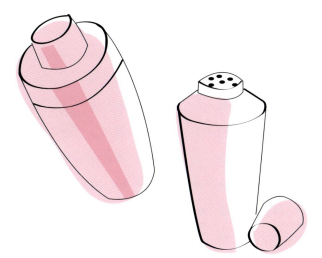

PIÑA COLADA

The most likely creator of this cocktail from Puerto Rico was Ramon Marrero, barman at the Caribe Hilton in the 1950s. Ideally, you should use crushed fresh fruit to give the drink that just-off-the-beach flavor.

Fresh Piña Colada

1 CUP CRUSHED ICE
3 oz WHITE RUM
2 oz COCONUT CREAM
3 TBSP CHOPPED PINEAPPLE
1 TSP SUGAR SYRUP (SEE PAGE 19)
WEDGE OF PINEAPPLE
Serve in: goblet or highball

Did you know?

Coconut cream is not the milk found inside fresh coconuts. It is a liquid made by simmering shredded coconut flesh in water. It is widely available in cans. You can also use coconut milk (which is made by the same method but contains more water) for a lighter flavor.

Ｙ Put the crushed ice in the blender.

Ｙ Pour in the rum and coconut cream.

Ｙ Add the chopped pineapple and the sugar syrup.

Ｙ Blend until smooth.

Ｙ Pour into a goblet or highball (do not strain).

Ｙ Decorate with the pineapple wedge and a single pineapple leaf.

Ｙ Serve with a straw.

Strawberry Colada

1 CUP CRUSHED ICE
3 oz WHITE RUM
3 oz PINEAPPLE JUICE
1 oz COCONUT CREAM
6 STRAWBERRIES, HULLED AND CHOPPED
PINEAPPLE WEDGE AND STRAWBERRY SLICES
Serve in: goblet or highball

Ｙ Add the crushed ice to a blender.

Ｙ Pour in the rum, pineapple juice, and coconut cream.

Ｙ Add the chopped strawberries.

Ｙ Blend until smooth.

Ｙ Pour into a goblet or highball (do not strain).

Ｙ Decorate with the pineapple wedge and strawberry slices.

For a **Pineapple Colada,** follow the recipe for the Fresh Piña Colada, but replace the chopped pineapple and the sugar syrup with 3 oz pineapple juice. Omit the straw.

Fresh Piña Colada

MANHATTAN

The Manhattan's appeal lies in its simplicity. There are just three ingredients: whiskey, vermouth, and bitters. A maraschino cherry adds the finishing touch.

As a rule, Manhattans are made with one part vermouth to three parts whiskey. Sweet vermouth is usually used to balance the dryness of the whiskey, while the bitters add a zesty tang. You can also use dry vermouth or an equal mixture of both.

The Manhattan is said to take its name from the New York club where it was invented at the behest of American socialite Jenny Jerome. She wanted a new drink to celebrate the election of Samuel J. Tilden as Governor of New York in 1874, and this was the bartender's offering. The Manhattan was not Jenny Jerome's only contribution to the world: that same year she gave birth to Winston Churchill.

Which whiskey?

Originally the Manhattan was made with American rye, but you can use whichever whiskey you like best. A Manhattan made with Scotch whisky is known as a Rob Roy.

Manhattan

3 oz WHISKEY
1 oz SWEET VERMOUTH
2–3 DROPS OF ANGOSTURA BITTERS
MARASCHINO CHERRY
Serve in: martini glass

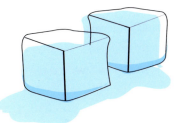

Y Add 4 or 5 ice cubes to a mixing glass.

Y Pour in the whiskey and vermouth.

Y Add the bitters and stir well to mix.

Y Strain into a martini glass.

Y Drop in the cherry.

Dry Manhattan

3 oz WHISKEY
1 oz DRY VERMOUTH
2–3 DROPS OF ANGOSTURA BITTERS
TWIST OF LEMON PEEL
Serve in: martini glass

Y Put 4 or 5 ice cubes into a mixing glass.

Y Add all the ingredients except the lemon twist.

Y Stir, then strain into a martini glass.

Y Decorate with the lemon twist.

Perfect Manhattan

3 oz WHISKEY
½ oz DRY VERMOUTH
½ oz SWEET VERMOUTH
2–3 DROPS OF ANGOSTURA BITTERS
MARASCHINO CHERRY
TWIST OF LEMON PEEL
Serve in: martini glass

Y Put 4 or 5 ice cubes in a mixing glass.

Y Pour in the whiskey and the vermouths.

Y Add the bitters.

Y Stir well, then strain into a martini glass.

Y Decorate with the cherry and lemon twist.

BLOODY MARY

The Bloody Mary was created in 1921 by Fernand Petiot, barman at Harry's New York Bar in Paris. He claimed the name was coined by a customer who said the color of the drink brought to mind Chicago's Bucket of Blood Club—and a girl called Mary whom he'd met there.

••

Bloody Mary

1½ oz VODKA
5 oz TOMATO JUICE
½ oz LEMON JUICE
2 DASHES OF WORCESTERSHIRE SAUCE
2–3 DROPS OF TABASCO SAUCE
PINCH OF CELERY SALT
TWIST OF BLACK PEPPER
STALK OF CELERY
TWIST OF LEMON OR LIME PEEL
Serve in: highball

℡ Fill a shaker with ice.

℡ Add the vodka, juices, Worcestershire sauce, and Tabasco.

℡ Shake, then strain into a highball filled with ice.

℡ Add the salt and pepper and decorate with the celery and lemon or lime twist.

••

Bullshot

1½ oz VODKA
5 oz BEEF CONSOMMÉ
½ oz LEMON JUICE
2 DASHES OF WORCESTERSHIRE SAUCE
2–3 DROPS OF TABASCO SAUCE
PINCH OF CELERY SALT
TWIST OF BLACK PEPPER
STALK OF CELERY
TWIST OF LEMON OR LIME PEEL
Serve in: highball

℡ Fill a shaker with ice.

℡ Add the vodka, consommé, lemon juice, Worcestershire sauce, and Tabasco.

℡ Shake, then strain into a highball filled with ice.

℡ Add the salt and pepper and decorate with the celery and lemon or lime twist.

For a **Bloody Maria,** follow the recipe for a Bloody Mary, but replace the vodka with the same quantity of tequila, then continue in the usual way.

Bloody Mary

STINGER

This is one of those very simple combinations that works perfectly. The sharp crème de menthe cuts through the smoothness of the brandy to create a sublime drink. It is best drunk after dinner—both brandy and crème de menthe help to settle the stomach—or as a nightcap. It is usually served neat, but you can have it on the rocks if you prefer.

We don't know who first dreamed up the Stinger, but it was well-known in the 1930s: American bartender Patrick Duffy included it in his *Official Mixer's Manual,* published in 1934. Both Evelyn Waugh and Somerset Maugham, those two chroniclers of England between the wars, were fond of the occasional stinger.

The Stinger is among the most adaptable of cocktails: try it with vodka, tequila, Amaretto, or Bailey's Irish Cream to replace the brandy. However, make sure that you use white crème de menthe, not green. And watch out: this cocktail really does have a powerful sting.

Stinger

2 oz BRANDY
⅔ oz **WHITE CRÈME DE MENTHE**
Serve in: martini glass

🍸 Half-fill a shaker with ice.
🍸 Pour in the brandy and crème de menthe.
🍸 Shake.
🍸 Strain into a martini glass.

Vodka Stinger

2 oz VODKA
1 oz WHITE CRÈME DE MENTHE
SPRIG OF MINT
Serve in: Old-fashioned glass

Y Fill an Old-fashioned glass with ice.

Y Pour in the vodka.

Y Add the crème de menthe.

Y Stir.

Y Decorate with the mint sprig.

Tequila Stinger

2 oz TEQUILA
1 oz WHITE CRÈME DE MENTHE
SPRIG OF MINT
Serve in: Old-fashioned glass

Y Fill an Old-fashioned glass with ice.

Y Pour in the tequila.

Y Add the crème de menthe.

Y Stir.

Y Decorate with the mint sprig.

Chocolate Stinger

1 oz CRÈME DE CACAO
1 oz WHITE CRÈME DE MENTHE
SPRIG OF MINT
Serve in: Old-fashioned glass

Y Fill an Old-fashioned glass with ice.

Y Pour in the crème de cacao.

Y Add the crème de menthe.

Y Stir.

Y Decorate with the mint sprig.

MARTINI

The precise recipe for the perfect Martini has been a subject of endless passionate debate. But one thing every aficionado agrees on is that a Martini must be served ice-cold. Keep the gin or vodka in the freezer, mix vigorously over ice, and chill the glasses for at least an hour before serving—your Martini should stay chilled to the last drop.

A true Martini consists of a large shot of gin with a dash of vermouth, but the original recipe mixed gin and vermouth in equal amounts. It is really a matter of taste: the smaller the dash of vermouth, the drier your Martini. But the latest Martini creators have abandoned the traditional gin base. Today, vodka rules (*see pages 86–103*).

Dry Martini

2 oz GIN
½ oz DRY VERMOUTH
COCKTAIL OLIVES, RINSED
Serve in: martini glass

- Fill a mixing glass with ice.
- Add the gin and vermouth and stir.
- Strain into a martini glass.
- Decorate with the olives.

New Orleans Martini

2–3 DROPS OF PERNOD
2 oz GIN
½ oz DRY VERMOUTH
COCKTAIL OLIVES, RINSED
Serve in: martini glass

- Fill a shaker or mixing glass with ice cubes.
- Add the Pernod.
- Pour in the gin and vermouth and stir.
- Strain into a martini glass.
- Decorate with the olives.

For a **Vodkatini,** follow the Dry Martini recipe, but replace the gin with the same quantity of vodka, and decorate with a twist of lemon peel, either instead of or in addition to an olive or two.

Dry Martini

Gibson

2 oz GIN
½ oz DRY VERMOUTH
2 COCKTAIL ONIONS
Serve in: martini glass

Y Add ice to a mixing glass.

Y Pour in the gin and vermouth.

Y Strain into a martini glass.

Y Decorate with the two onions on a toothpick.

Dirty Martini

2 oz GIN
½ oz DRY VERMOUTH
2 TSP LIQUID FROM JAR OF COCKTAIL OLIVES
COCKTAIL OLIVE, RINSED
Serve in: martini glass

Y Fill a shaker with ice.

Y Pour in the gin and vermouth.

Y Add the olive liquid.

Y Shake well.

Y Strain into a martini glass.

Y Decorate with the cocktail olive.

Did you know?

Cheers! Franklin Delano Roosevelt drank a Dirty Martini to celebrate the end of Prohibition in 1933.

Tequilatini

2 oz WHITE TEQUILA
½ oz DRY VERMOUTH
TWIST OF LEMON PEEL
Serve in: martini glass

Y Fill a mixing glass with ice.

Y Add the tequila and vermouth.

Y Stir.

Y Strain into a martini glass.

Y Decorate with the lemon twist.

Spirits

There is barely a fruit, a vegetable, or a grain that has not been turned into an alcoholic drink at some time or another somewhere in the world. But as far as cocktails are concerned, there are six noble spirits: gin, vodka, tequila, rum, whiskey, and brandy. These spirits, when mixed with liqueurs, juices, and other concoctions, form the basis of the vast range of amusing, exciting, and surprising drinks we call cocktails.

GIN

Gin is the foundation of hundreds of cocktails, including the eternal Martini. Its distinctive taste comes from juniper berries. The very word gin is a short form of the Dutch word *genever*, meaning "juniper."

Even today there are two basic types of gin—Dutch and English. Dutch gin contains malted rye, which gives the drink a pungent, rustic taste that is slightly reminiscent of whiskey. The best-known brand is Bols.

English gin, which is distilled predominantly from corn, has a drier, sharper taste, and tends to be stronger than the Dutch variant. London Dry, the most popular, includes well-known brands such as Gordon's, Booth's, and Bombay Sapphire; Plymouth gin is drier. English gin has a delicate taste that goes well with most mixers, including tonic, bitter lemon, and fruit juices. You can serve it neat, but be sure it is ice-cold.

Gin was a horribly rough brew in the 18th century, nothing more than homebrew hooch. Heavy taxes and government controls put many distillers out of business, with the result that gin went upmarket over the next century. It evolved into the dry, clear drink we know today as London Dry.

Military men and civil servants took the new spirit all over the Empire. These expatriates, at their malaria-ridden outposts in India, found that their medicinal dose of quinine in tonic was much more palatable when mixed with a splash of gin. So it was the British raj who gave the world the G&T (Gin and Tonic), one of the all-time great drinks.

Pink Gin

2 oz GIN (PREFERABLY PLYMOUTH)
DASH OF ANGOSTURA BITTERS
SPLASH OF ICE WATER (OPTIONAL)
Serve in: martini glass

Y Fill a mixing glass with ice.

Y Pour in the gin.

Y Add the bitters.

Y Stir to mix.

Y Strain into a martini glass and serve with the water, if using.

Gimlet

2 oz GIN
1 oz LIME CORDIAL
SLICE OF LIME
Serve in: Old-fashioned glass

Y Fill an Old-fashioned glass
  with ice.

Y Pour in the gin and cordial.

Y Stir.

Y Drop in the lime slice.

Did you know?
This drink was traditionally made with Plymouth gin, which is drier than most London Dry gins.

Gin Sour

2 oz GIN
1 oz LEMON JUICE
1 TSP SUPERFINE SUGAR
DASH OF CLUB SODA (OPTIONAL)
Serve in: Old-fashioned glass

Y Fill a shaker with ice.

Y Add all the ingredients except the club soda.

Y Shake well.

Y Strain into an Old-fashioned glass.

Y Add the dash of club soda, if using.

Gin Cocktail

2 oz GIN
2 DASHES OF ANGOSTURA BITTERS
TWIST OF LEMON PEEL
Serve in: martini glass

Y Fill a mixing glass with ice.

Y Add the gin and bitters.

Y Stir well.

Y Strain into a martini glass.

Y Decorate with the lemon twist.

Bartender's tip
Try this with orange bitters and decorate with a twist of orange peel.

Gin and It

1 oz GIN
1 oz SWEET VERMOUTH
MARASCHINO CHERRY
TWIST OF ORANGE PEEL
Serve in: Old-fashioned glass

Y Add 3 or 4 ice cubes to an Old-fashioned glass.

Y Pour in the gin and sweet vermouth.

Y Stir.

Y Decorate with the cherry and orange twist.

Bee's Knees

1½ oz GIN
2 TSP HONEY
1 TSP LEMON JUICE
Serve in: martini glass

Y Fill a shaker with ice.

Y Add the gin, honey, and lemon juice.

Y Shake well, so that the honey is well mixed in.

Y Strain into a martini glass.

Gin and Tonic

2 oz GIN
4 oz TONIC WATER
SLICE OF LEMON
Serve in: highball

Y Fill a highball with ice.

Y Pour in the gin.

Y Top off with the tonic water.

Y Stir.

Y Drop in the lemon slice.

Gin Rickey

2 oz GIN
½ oz LIME JUICE
1 TSP SUPERFINE SUGAR
CLUB SODA
WEDGE OF LIME
Serve in: highball

Y Fill a shaker with ice.

Y Add the gin, lime juice, and sugar.

Y Shake well and strain into a highball.

Y Top off with club soda.

Y Decorate with the lime wedge.

Gin Sling

2 oz GIN
2 oz LEMON JUICE
1 TSP SUPERFINE SUGAR
CLUB SODA
TWIST OF LEMON PEEL
Serve in: Old-fashioned glass

Y Fill a shaker with ice.

Y Add the gin, lemon juice, and sugar.

Y Shake well.

Y Strain into an ice-filled Old-fashioned glass.

Y Top off with club soda.

Y Stir again.

Y Decorate with the lemon twist.

Gin Highball

2 oz GIN
SPARKLING MINERAL WATER
TWIST OF LEMON PEEL
Serve in: highball

Y Fill a highball with ice.

Y Pour in the gin.

Y Top off with mineral water.

Y Drop in the lemon twist.

Horse's Neck

PEEL OF 1 LEMON, CUT IN A SPIRAL
2 oz GIN
½ oz LEMON JUICE
GINGER ALE
Serve in: highball

Bartender's tip
To make the spiral, start at the stem end of the lemon and cut a continuous ½-in strip of the whole peel.

Ȳ Hang the lemon spiral over the edge of the
  highball, so that most of it is inside
  the glass.

Ȳ Fill the glass with ice.

Ȳ Add the gin and lemon juice.

Ȳ Stir.

Ȳ Top off with the ginger ale.

Ȳ Stir again.

Gin Smash

1 TSP SUPERFINE SUGAR
5 SPRIGS OF MINT
DASH OF HOT WATER
2 oz GIN
1 oz CLUB SODA
SLICE OF ORANGE
Serve in: Old-fashioned glass

Ȳ Place the sugar and the leaves from 4 of the mint sprigs in an
  Old-fashioned glass.

Ȳ Add the water.

Ȳ Muddle, or crush with the back of a spoon, to dissolve the sugar
  and bruise the mint leaves.

Ȳ Add 3 or 4 ice cubes to the glass.

Ȳ Pour in the gin and club soda.

Ȳ Stir.

Ȳ Decorate with the remaining mint sprig and the orange slice.

Orange Blossom

2 oz GIN
4 oz ORANGE JUICE
1–2 DROPS OF ANGOSTURA BITTERS
SLICE OF ORANGE
SPRIG OF MINT
Serve in: highball

Ϋ Fill a shaker with ice.

Ϋ Pour in the gin and orange juice.

Ϋ Add the bitters.

Ϋ Shake.

Ϋ Strain into a highball filled with ice.

Ϋ Decorate with the orange slice and mint sprig.

Pink Pussycat

2 oz GIN
2 oz PINEAPPLE JUICE
2 oz GRAPEFRUIT JUICE
DASH OF GRENADINE
WEDGE OF PINEAPPLE
Serve in: Old-fashioned glass

Ϋ Fill a shaker with ice.

Ϋ Add the gin, juices, and grenadine.

Ϋ Shake.

Ϋ Strain into an Old-fashioned glass.

Ϋ Decorate with the grapefruit wedge.

Daisy

2 oz GIN
1 oz LEMON JUICE
1 oz ORANGE JUICE
1 TSP GRENADINE
MARASCHINO CHERRY
SLICE OF ORANGE
Serve in: Old-fashioned glass

Y Fill a shaker with ice.

Y Add the gin, juices, and grenadine.

Y Shake.

Y Strain into an Old-fashioned glass.

Y Decorate with the cherry and orange slice.

UFO

2 oz GENEVER (DUTCH GIN)
BITTER LEMON
SLICE OF LEMON
Serve in: highball

Y Fill a highball with ice.

Y Add the genever.

Y Top off with bitter lemon.

Y Decorate with the lemon slice.

Waikiki Beach

2 oz GIN
½ oz DRY VERMOUTH
1 oz PINEAPPLE JUICE
1 oz LEMON JUICE
WEDGE OF PINEAPPLE
Serve in: Old-fashioned glass

Y Fill a shaker with ice.

Y Pour in the gin, vermouth, and juices.

Y Shake.

Y Strain into an Old-fashioned glass.

Y Decorate with the pineapple wedge.

Clover Club

2 oz GIN
⅔ oz LIME JUICE
½ TSP SUPERFINE SUGAR
½ EGG WHITE
Serve in: martini glass

Y Fill a shaker with ice.

Y Add the gin, lime juice, sugar, and egg white.

Y Shake well, until the egg white is thoroughly mixed in.

Y Strain into a martini glass.

. . . .

Pink Clover Club

2 oz GIN
⅔ oz LIME JUICE
½ TSP SUPERFINE SUGAR
DASH OF GRENADINE
½ EGG WHITE
Serve in: martini glass

Y Fill a cocktail shaker with ice.

Y Add the gin, lime juice, sugar, grenadine, and egg white.

Y Shake well, until the egg white is thoroughly mixed in.

Y Strain into a martini glass.

. . . .

Jockey Club

2 oz GIN
½ oz AMARETTO
½ oz LEMON JUICE
DASH OF ANGOSTURA BITTERS
HALF-SLICE OF LEMON
Serve in: martini glass

Y Fill a shaker with ice.

Y Pour in the gin, Amaretto, and lemon juice.

Y Add the bitters.

Y Shake.

Y Strain into a martini glass.

Y Decorate with the lemon.

Negroni

¾ oz **CAMPARI**
1 oz **SWEET VERMOUTH**
2 oz **GIN**
CLUB SODA
TWIST OF LEMON
Serve in: Old-fashioned glass

Ï Add 2 or 3 ice cubes to an Old-fashioned glass.

Ï Pour in the Campari, vermouth, and gin.

Ï Stir.

Ï Top off with club soda.

Ï Stir again.

Ï Decorate with the lemon twist.

Did you know?

The Negroni was invented in the 1920s by an Italian count—Conte Camillo Negroni. His favorite cocktail was the Americano, but he wanted a drier taste so he added gin to the traditional mix of Campari and vermouth. The result was this sophisticated aperitif. The Negroni is usually made with sweet vermouth, but you can make it with dry if you prefer. It also works well if you use vodka instead of the gin.

Negroni

Tod's Cooler

2 oz GIN
½ oz CRÈME DE CASSIS
½ oz LEMON JUICE
CLUB SODA
WEDGE OF LEMON
Serve in: highball

🍸 Fill a shaker with ice.

🍸 Add the gin, crème de cassis, and lemon juice.

🍸 Shake.

🍸 Strain into a highball filled with ice.

🍸 Top off with club soda.

🍸 Stir.

🍸 Decorate with the lemon wedge.

Bramble

2 oz GIN
1 oz LIME JUICE
1 TSP SUPERFINE SUGAR
½ oz CRÈME DE MÛRE
2 WHOLE BLACKBERRIES
SLICE OF LEMON
Serve in: Old-fashioned glass

🍸 Fill a shaker with ice.

🍸 Add the gin, lime juice, and sugar.

🍸 Shake.

🍸 Strain into an Old-fashioned glass two-thirds filled with crushed ice.

🍸 Pour in the crème de mûre.

🍸 Decorate with the blackberries and lemon slice.

Maiden's Prayer

1 oz GIN
1 oz COINTREAU
½ oz FRESH ORANGE JUICE
½ oz FRESH LEMON JUICE
TWIST OF ORANGE PEEL
Serve in: cocktail glass

Ⴤ Fill a shaker with ice.

Ⴤ Add the gin, cointreau, and juices.

Ⴤ Shake.

Ⴤ Strain into a cocktail glass.

Ⴤ Decorate with the orange twist.

• •

RAC

2 oz GIN
1 oz DRY VERMOUTH
1 oz SWEET RED VERMOUTH
2–3 DROPS GRENADINE
2–3 DROPS ORANGE BITTERS
TWIST OF ORANGE PEEL
Serve in: martini glass

Ⴤ Fill a mixing glass with ice.

Ⴤ Pour in the gin, dry vermouth,
and sweet vermouth.

Ⴤ Add the grenadine and bitters.

Ⴤ Stir well.

Ⴤ Strain into a martini glass.

Ⴤ Drop in the orange twist.

Did you know?
This drink was created at the Royal Automobile Club in London on the outbreak of the First World War.

Southern Seas

1 oz GIN
½ oz GALLIANO
LEMONADE
½ oz BLUE CURAÇAO
WEDGE OF LEMON
Serve in: highball

Ϋ Fill a shaker with ice.

Ϋ Add the gin and Galliano.

Ϋ Shake.

Ϋ Pour into a highball filled with ice.

Ϋ Top off with lemonade.

Ϋ Stir lightly.

Ϋ Pour in the blue curaçao.

Ϋ Decorate with the lemon wedge.

> **Bartender's tip**
> Pour the blue curaçao slowly into the glass so that it sinks to the bottom, creating a gorgeous two-tone drink. Serve with a straw.

Gin Alexander

1 oz GIN
1 oz WHITE CRÈME DE CACAO
1 oz HEAVY CREAM
SMALL PIECE OF SEMISWEET CHOCOLATE, GRATED
Serve in: martini glass

Ϋ Fill a shaker with ice.

Ϋ Add the gin, crème de cacao, and cream.

Ϋ Shake well, so that the cream is thoroughly mixed in.

Ϋ Strain into a martini glass.

Ϋ Top with grated chocolate.

Southern Seas

Monkey Gland

2 oz GIN
1 oz ORANGE JUICE
2 TSP GRENADINE
1 TSP PERNOD
SLICE OF ORANGE

Serve in: martini glass

Y Fill a shaker with ice.

Y Add all the ingredients except
the orange.

Y Shake.

Y Strain into a martini glass.

Y Decorate with the orange slice.

Did you know?

Cheers! This cocktail has been
around since the 1920s. It was
invented at the London Ciro's Club
by Harry McElhone—creator of the
Sidecar *(see page 40)* and the White
Lady *(see page 28)*.

Chinese Dragon

1½ oz GIN
½ oz COINTREAU
¾ oz MANDARIN JUICE
2 MANDARIN SEGMENTS

Serve in: Old-fashioned glass

Y Fill a shaker with ice.

Y Add the gin, Cointreau, and
mandarin juice.

Y Pour into an old-fashioned
glass (do not strain).

Y Decorate with the mandarin
segments.

Bartender's tip
*Use freshly squeezed
mandarin juice if
possible; otherwise,
you can use the
juice from a can of
mandarin segments.*

Casanova

1 oz **GIN**
¾ oz **COINTREAU**
½ oz **APRICOT BRANDY**
2 oz **PASSION FRUIT JUICE**
2 oz **PINEAPPLE JUICE**
WEDGE OF PINEAPPLE

Serve in: highball

Y Fill a shaker with ice.

Y Add all the ingredients except the pineapple wedge.

Y Shake.

Y Strain into a highball filled with ice.

Y Decorate with the pineapple wedge.

Knockout

2 oz **GIN**
1 oz **DRY VERMOUTH**
½ oz **WHITE CRÈME DE MENTHE**
2 DROPS OF PERNOD
SLICE OF LEMON

Serve in: martini glass

Y Fill a mixing glass with ice.

Y Add the gin, vermouth, and crème de menthe.

Y Stir well.

Y Strain into a martini glass.

Y Drop in the Pernod.

Y Decorate with the lemon slice.

VODKA

"Vodka" is a Russian word that means "little water." In eastern Europe it is almost always drunk neat, but the fact that it is a pure spirit, devoid of any color or flavoring, makes vodka the perfect base for cocktails. You can add it to absolutely anything to impart an alcoholic kick. Two of the most highly prized brands of Russian vodka are Stolichnaya and Smirnoff, but other chilly countries—notably Finland and Poland— also produce high-class brands of this most versatile of spirits.

Vodka, though colorless and flavorless, comes in many varieties and degrees of smoothness. The best vodkas hit the back of the throat and then give a pleasing warm sensation that spreads through the chest. There are also many vodka infusions, which are made by adding berries, herbs, or other substances to create flavored drinks. Some of the most popular are lemon vodka (*limonovka*), cranberry vodka (known as *klyukovka*), bison grass vodka (called *zubrovka* in Poland), and most fiery of all, pepper vodka (*pertsovka,* a popular drink in the bitterly cold wilderness of Siberia), which is made by adding chilies to a bottle and leaving it for six months or so.

Among the best-known vodka-based cocktails are the Moscow Mule and Black Russian. But vodka is also the base for the latest Martinis to be mixed by imaginative bartenders. They include Chocolate Martini (vanilla vodka and chocolate liqueur); Tropical (Malibu, vanilla vodka, and pineapple juice); The Thin Mint (vodka, white crème de cacao, and green crème de menthe); the Mudslide (vodka, Bailey's and Kahlúa); and the Apple (vodka, apple pucker, and sour mix).

Vodka Gimlet

2 oz VODKA
1 oz LIME CORDIAL
SLICE OF LIME
Serve in: Old-fashioned glass

Ⓨ Fill an Old-fashioned glass with ice.

Ⓨ Pour in the vodka and cordial.

Ⓨ Stir.

Ⓨ Drop in the lime slice.

Bartender's tip
Try this with lime vodka for extra zest. You can also sweeten it by adding a teaspoon of sugar syrup (see page 19).

Vodka Sour

2 oz VODKA
1 oz LEMON JUICE
1 TSP SUPERFINE SUGAR
CLUB SODA
Serve in: Old-fashioned glass

Ⓨ Fill a shaker with ice.

Ⓨ Add all the ingredients except the club soda and shake well.

Ⓨ Strain into an Old-fashioned glass.

Ⓨ Top off with club soda.

Ⓨ Stir.

In the Pink

DASH OF ANGOSTURA BITTERS
2 oz VODKA
ICE WATER (OPTIONAL)
Serve in: Old-fashioned glass

Ⓨ Drop the bitters into an Old-fashioned glass and roll around to coat the sides.

Ⓨ Pour in the vodka.

Ⓨ Add ice water to taste, if using.

Vodka Twister

3 oz VODKA
3 DROPS PERNOD
2 oz LEMON JUICE
1 TSP SUPERFINE SUGAR
1 EGG WHITE
DRY GINGER ALE
TWIST OF LEMON PEEL
Serve in: highball

♟ Fill a shaker with ice.

♟ Add the vodka, Pernod, lemon juice, sugar, and egg white.

♟ Shake well until the egg white is fully mixed in.

♟ Strain into a highball filled with ice.

♟ Top off with ginger ale.

♟ Stir.

♟ Decorate with the lemon twist.

• •

Harvey Wallbanger

1 oz VODKA
4 oz ORANGE JUICE
½ oz GALLIANO
SLICE OF ORANGE
Serve in: highball

♟ Fill a highball with ice.

♟ Pour in the vodka and orange juice.

♟ Stir.

Did you know?

So-calleded because it was the favorite drink of a surfer named Harvey, who is alleged to have imbibed so many of them one day that he started banging his head against a wall.

♟ Slowly pour the Galliano over the back of a spoon so that it floats on top of the drink.

♟ Drop in the orange slice.

Balalaika

2 oz VODKA
1 oz COINTREAU
1 oz LEMON JUICE
SLICE OF ORANGE OR LEMON
MARASCHINO OR FRESH CHERRY
Serve in: martini glass

Y Fill a shaker with ice.

Y Add the vodka, Cointreau, and lemon juice.

Y Shake.

Y Strain into a martini glass.

Y Decorate with the orange/lemon slice and cherry.

What's in a name?

This delicious cocktail has wonderful citrus flavors. It is a classic combination from the 1930s when vodka cocktails were often given Russian names in honor of the mother country. A balalaika is a little musical instrument, like a three-stringed banjo, which provides the accompaniment to melancholy Russian folk songs.

Vodka Zaza

2 oz VODKA
1 oz DUBONNET
3 DROPS ANGOSTURA BITTERS
Serve in: martini glass

Y Fill a shaker with ice.

Y Add the vodka and Dubonnet.

Y Drop in the bitters.

Y Shake.

Y Strain into a martini glass.

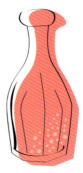

For a **Blue Balalaika,** add 1 oz blue curaçao. Another modern twist is to use lime juice in place of the lemon—in which case the cocktail is called a **Kamikaze**. You can use lemon vodka in any of these drinks.

Balalaika

White Russian

2 oz VODKA
1 oz KAHLÚA
1 oz LIGHT CREAM
Serve in: martini glass

℗ Fill a shaker with ice.

℗ Add all the ingredients.

℗ Shake well, so that the cream is fully mixed in.

℗ Pour into a martini glass.

Vodka Cappuccino

2 oz VODKA
½ oz KAHLÚA
1 oz ESPRESSO (HOT)
1 oz LIGHT CREAM
1 TSP SUPERFINE SUGAR
SMALL PIECE OF SEMISWEET CHOCOLATE
Serve in: martini glass

℗ Fill a shaker with ice.

℗ Add the vodka, Kahlúa, espresso, cream, and sugar.

℗ Shake well, so that the cream is fully mixed in.

℗ Strain into a martini glass.

℗ Grate or flake the chocolate over the top.

Black Russian

1½ oz **VODKA**

¾ oz **KAHLÚA**

Serve in: Old-fashioned glass

Ï Pour the vodka into an Old-fashioned glass over ice.

Ï Add the Kahlúa.

Ï Stir.

• •

Long Black Russian

1½ oz **VODKA**

¾ oz **KAHLÚA**

COLA

Serve in: highball

Ï Fill a highball with ice.

Ï Pour in the vodka and Kahlúa.

Ï Top off with cola.

Did you know?

Because it is so neutral, vodka doesn't fight strong flavors such as coffee. The most famous vodka-coffee combination is the punchy Black Russian—but there are plenty of more mellow variations to try. You can use Tia Maria in place of the Kahlúa if you like.

Screwdriver

1 oz VODKA
2 oz ORANGE JUICE
DASH OF ANGOSTURA BITTERS (OPTIONAL)
Serve in: Old-fashioned glass

Ÿ Fill an Old-fashioned glass with ice cubes.

Ÿ Pour in the vodka and orange juice.

Ÿ Add the bitters, if using.

Ÿ Stir.

Vodka Silver Fizz

2 oz LEMON VODKA
1½ oz LEMON JUICE
1 TSP SUPERFINE SUGAR
½ EGG WHITE
CLUB SODA
WEDGE OF LEMON
Serve in: highball

Ÿ Fill a shaker with ice.

Ÿ Pour in the vodka and lemon juice.

Ÿ Add the sugar and egg white.

Ÿ Shake well until the egg white is completely mixed in.

Ÿ Strain into a highball filled with ice.

Ÿ Top off with club soda.

Ÿ Decorate with the lemon wedge.

Vodka Sling

2 oz VODKA
2 oz LEMON JUICE
1 TSP SUPERFINE SUGAR
CLUB SODA
SLICE OF LEMON
Serve in: Old-fashioned glass

℣ Fill a shaker with ice.

℣ Add the vodka, lemon juice, and sugar.

℣ Shake well.

℣ Strain into an ice-filled Old-fashioned glass.

℣ Top off with club soda.

℣ Stir again.

℣ Drop in the lemon slice.

Island Vodka Sling

3 oz VODKA
1 oz BRANDY
1 oz LEMON JUICE
1 oz ORANGE JUICE
3 DROPS ANGOSTURA BITTERS
CLUB SODA
SLICE OF ORANGE
Serve in: highball

℣ Fill a shaker with ice.

℣ Add all the ingredients except the club soda and orange slice.

℣ Shake.

℣ Strain into a highball filled with ice.

℣ Top off with club soda.

℣ Stir.

℣ Decorate with the orange slice.

Cosmopolitan

1 oz VODKA
½ oz COINTREAU
1 oz CRANBERRY JUICE
½ oz LIME JUICE
TWIST OF ORANGE OR LEMON PEEL
Serve in: martini glass

> **Bartender's tip**
> *This one tastes even better if you use a cranberry-flavored vodka.*

⏃ Fill a shaker with ice.

⏃ Add the vodka, Cointreau, cranberry juice, and lime juice.

⏃ Shake.

⏃ Strain into a martini glass.

⏃ Drop in the orange/lemon twist.

••

Pearl Harbor

1 oz VODKA
½ oz MIDORI
1 oz PINEAPPLE JUICE
Serve in: martini glass

⏃ Fill a shaker with ice.

⏃ Pour in the vodka, Midori, and pineapple juice.

⏃ Shake, then strain into a martini glass.

••

Velvet Hammer

2 oz VODKA
½ oz WHITE CRÈME DE CACAO
½ oz LIGHT CREAM
SMALL PIECE OF SEMISWEET CHOCOLATE
Serve in: martini glass

⏃ Fill a shaker with ice.

⏃ Add the vodka, crème de cacao, and cream.

⏃ Shake well, so that the cream is thoroughly mixed in.

⏃ Strain into a martini glass.

⏃ Grate the chocolate over the top.

Cosmopolitan

French Martini

2 oz VODKA
½ oz CHAMBORD OR CRÈME DE FRAMBOISE
1 oz PINEAPPLE JUICE
TWIST OF ORANGE PEEL

Serve in: martini glass

℣ Fill a shaker with ice.

℣ Pour in the vodka, Chambord or crème de framboise, and pineapple juice.

℣ Shake.

℣ Strain into a martini glass.

℣ Decorate with the orange twist.

French Horn

2 oz VODKA
1 oz CHAMBORD
½ oz LEMON JUICE
1 WHOLE RASPBERRY

Serve in: martini glass

℣ Fill a mixing glass with ice.

℣ Add all the ingredients except the fresh raspberry.

℣ Stir.

℣ Strain into a martini glass.

℣ Decorate with the raspberry.

Did you know?

Chambord is a French black raspberry liqueur. You can substitute crème de framboise if you like.

French Kiss

2 oz VODKA
½ oz CHAMBORD OR CRÈME DE FRAMBOISE
½ oz CRÈME DE CACAO
½ oz LIGHT CREAM

Serve in: martini glass

℣ Fill a shaker with ice.

℣ Add all the ingredients.

℣ Shake.

℣ Strain into a martini glass.

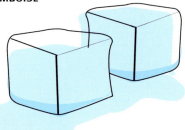

Chocolate Martini

1½ oz VANILLA VODKA
1 oz GODIVA CHOCOLATE LIQUEUR
1 CHERRY
Serve in: martini glass

Y Add ice to a mixing glass.

Y Pour in the vodka and chocolate liqueur.

Y Strain into a martini glass.

Y Decorate with the cherry.

Pomegranate Martini

2 oz CITRUS VODKA
½ oz FRESH LEMON JUICE
¼ oz FRESH POMEGRANTE JUICE
1 oz SUGAR SYRUP
TWIST OF ORANGE PEEL
Serve in: martini glass

Y Add ice to a mixing glass.

Y Pour in the vodka, juices and syrup.

Y Strain into a martini glass.

Y Decorate with the twist of orange peel.

Watermelon Martini

1 oz CITRUS VODKA
½ oz FRESH LEMON JUICE
1½ oz FRESH WATERMELON JUICE
1 oz MIDORI
SPRING OF MINT
Serve in: martini glass

Y Add ice to a mixing glass.

Y Pour in the vodka, juices and midori.

Y Strain into a martini glass.

Y Decorate with the sprig of mint.

Sour Apple Martini

1 oz VODKA
1 oz SOUR APPLE PUCKER
½ oz COINTREAU
TWIST OF LEMON PEEL
Serve in: martini glass

Ⓨ Add ice to a shaker mixing glass.

Ⓨ Pour in the vodka, the pucker, and Cointreau.

Ⓨ Stir.

Ⓨ Strain into a martini glass.

Ⓨ Decorate with the lemon twist.

Salty Dog

LEMON WEDGE
FINE SEA SALT
2 oz VODKA
5 oz GRAPEFRUIT JUICE
TWIST OF GRAPEFRUIT PEEL
Serve in: highball

Ⓨ Rub the rim of a highball with the lemon wedge.

Ⓨ Dip the rim in a saucer filled with fine sea salt.

Ⓨ Fill a shaker with ice.

Ⓨ Pour in the vodka and grapefruit juice.

Ⓨ Shake.

Ⓨ Strain into the salt-rimmed glass.

Ⓨ Drop in the grapefruit twist.

Did you know?

This cocktail was originally made with gin rather than vodka. Either way, it is a good aperitif.

Sea Breeze

2 oz VODKA
2 oz GRAPEFRUIT JUICE
3 oz CRANBERRY JUICE
WEDGE OF LIME
3–4 CRANBERRIES
Serve in: highball

- Fill a shaker with ice.
- Add the vodka and juices.
- Shake.
- Strain into a highball filled with ice.
- Decorate with a lime wedge and the cranberries speared on a toothpick.

Warm Breeze

2 oz VODKA
1 oz PEACH SCHNAPPS
3 oz CRANBERRY JUICE
2 oz PINEAPPLE JUICE
WEDGE OF LIME
Serve in: highball

- Fill a shaker with ice.
- Add the vodka, Schnapps, and juices.
- Shake.
- Strain into a highball filled with ice.
- Decorate with the lime wedge.

Red Panties Martini

1 oz VODKA
½ oz PEACH SCHNAPPS
DASH OF GRENADINE
TWIST OF LEMON PEEL
Serve in: martini glass

- Add ice to a shaker mixing glass.
- Pour in the vodka, schnapps, and grenadine.
- Stir.
- Strain into a martini glass.
- Decorate with the lemon twist.

Vodka Negroni

½ oz **CAMPARI**

1 oz **SWEET VERMOUTH**

2 oz **VODKA**

CLUB SODA

SLICE OF ORANGE

Serve in: Old-fashioned glass

Ⓨ Add 2 or 3 ice cubes to an Old-fashioned glass.

Ⓨ Pour in the Campari, vermouth, and vodka.

Ⓨ Stir.

Ⓨ Top off with club soda.

Ⓨ Decorate with the orange slice.

Orange Mist

1 oz **VODKA**

1 oz **WHISKEY**

1 oz **ORANGE JUICE**

CLUB SODA

SLICE OF ORANGE

Serve in: Old-fashioned glass

Ⓨ Shake the vodka, whiskey, and juice in a shaker filled with ice.

Ⓨ Strain into an Old-fashioned glass.

Ⓨ Top off with club soda.

Ⓨ Decorate with the orange slice.

Green Eyes

2 oz VODKA
1 oz BLUE CURAÇAO
1 oz ORANGE JUICE
TWIST OF ORANGE PEEL
Serve in: martini glass

- Fill a shaker with ice.
- Add the vodka, curaçao, and juice.
- Shake.
- Strain into a martini glass.
- Decorate with the orange twist.

Blue Lagoon

2 oz VODKA
½ oz BLUE CURAÇAO
4 oz LEMONADE
SLICE OF ORANGE
MARASCHINO CHERRY
Serve in: highball

- Fill a mixing glass with ice.
- Add all the ingredients except the orange slice and cherry.
- Stir well.
- Strain into a highball filled with ice.
- Decorate with the orange slice and cherry.

Liquid Gold

2 oz VODKA
½ oz GALLIANO
½ oz CRÈME DE BANANE
1 oz ORANGE JUICE
TWIST OF ORANGE PEEL
Serve in: martini glass

- Fill a shaker with ice.
- Add all the ingredients except the orange twist.
- Shake.
- Strain into a martini glass.
- Decorate with the orange twist.

TEQUILA

Tequila is made by distilling the fermented juice of the blue agave plant. It used to have a reputation as a rough spirit, but now sophisticated, high-quality brands of tequila are widely available.

Tequila can be produced only in specific parts of Mexico, and by law it has to contain at least 51 percent agave. The more agave a tequila contains, the better the quality: the best tequilas are 100 percent agave.

There are various types of tequila. Silver or white tequila is bottled straight after distillation, and is clear, like vodka. It is usually served with fruit juices, and its fresh, clean flavor goes well with salt. This is why that most famous of tequila cocktails, the Margarita (*see page 26*), which contains lime juice, is served with a salted rim.

Gold tequila gets its color either from the addition of caramel, or from being aged in oak casks. The smoothest tequilas stay in casks for up to four years—they are called *anejo* (the Spanish word for old). But many people prefer *reposado* (meaning rested) tequilas, which are aged for between eight weeks and twelve months—just long enough to smooth out the sharpness of the agave.

Generally speaking, anejo and reposado tequilas are drunk neat. But reposado tequila also goes well in some cocktails, or can be served alongside a spicy tomato chaser called a Sangrita (*see page 111*).

The cocktails in this section are made with silver (white) tequila unless otherwise specified.

Tequila Sour

2 oz TEQUILA
½ oz LEMON JUICE
1 TSP SUPERFINE SUGAR

Serve in: Old-fashioned glass

- Fill a shaker with ice.
- Add all the ingredients.
- Shake well.
- Strain into an Old-fashioned glass.

Viva Villa

LIME WEDGE
SUPERFINE SUGAR
2 oz TEQUILA
1 oz LIME JUICE
½ oz LEMON JUICE

Serve in: martini glass

- Rub the lime wedge over the rim of the glass.
- Dip in a saucer of the sugar to coat.
- Fill a shaker with ice.
- Add the tequila, lime juice, and lemon juice.
- Shake.
- Strain into a martini glass.

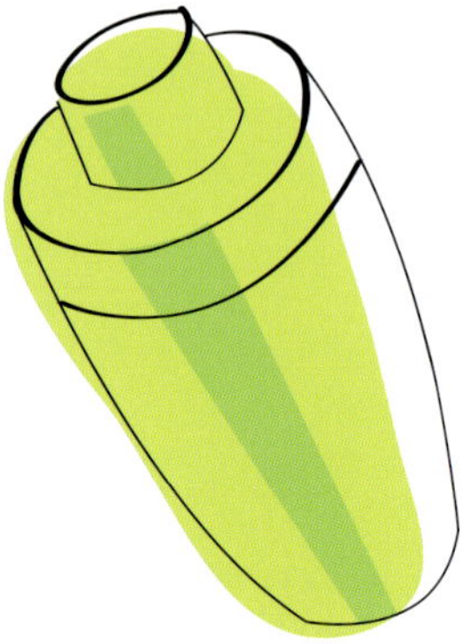

Tequila Fizz

2 oz TEQUILA
1 oz LIME JUICE
DASH OF ORANGE BITTERS
1 TSP SUPERFINE SUGAR
2 oz SPARKLING WATER
SLICE OF ORANGE
Serve in: highball

- Fill a shaker with ice.
- Add the tequila, lime juice, bitters, and sugar.
- Shake well.
- Strain into a highball filled with ice.
- Top off with the sparkling water.
- Decorate with the orange slice.

Mexicola

2 oz TEQUILA
½ oz LIME JUICE
COLA
SLICE OF LIME
Serve in: highball

- Fill a highball with ice.
- Add the tequila and lime juice.
- Stir.
- Top off with cola.
- Stir again.
- Drop in the lime slice.

Tequila Matador

1½ oz TEQUILA
3 oz PINEAPPLE JUICE
½ oz LIME JUICE
WEDGE OF LIME
Serve in: Old-fashioned glass

- Fill a shaker with ice.
- Add the tequila and juices.
- Shake.
- Strain into an Old-fashioned glass.
- Decorate with the lime wedge.

Tequila Breeze

2 oz TEQUILA
2 oz GRAPEFRUIT JUICE
1 oz CRANBERRY JUICE
CLUB SODA
WEDGE OF GRAPEFRUIT
Serve in: highball

- Fill a shaker with ice.
- Pour in the tequila and grapefruit juice.
- Shake.
- Strain into a highball filled with ice.
- Top off with club soda and stir again.
- Decorate with the grapefruit wedge.

Tequila Matador

Mexican Wave

2 oz TEQUILA
1 oz LEMON JUICE
1 TSP SUPERFINE SUGAR
DASH OF ANGOSTURA BITTERS
TONIC WATER
SLICE OF LIME
Serve in: highball

℞ Fill a shaker with ice.

℞ Add the tequila, lemon juice, sugar, and bitters.

℞ Strain into a highball filled with ice.

℞ Top off with tonic water.

℞ Stir.

℞ Drop in the lime slice.

Mexican Madras

1 oz GOLD TEQUILA
3 oz CRANBERRY JUICE
1 oz ORANGE JUICE
½ oz LIME JUICE
SLICE OF ORANGE
Serve in: highball

℞ Fill a shaker with ice.

℞ Add the tequila, cranberry juice, orange juice, and lime juice.

℞ Shake.

℞ Strain into a highball.

℞ Drop in the orange slice.

Sangrita Chaser

10 oz ORANGE JUICE
8 oz TOMATO JUICE
3 oz LIME JUICE
2 TBSP GRENADINE
½ TSP SALT
1 CHILI, FINELY CHOPPED
5–6 DROPS WORCESTERSHIRE SAUCE
BLACK PEPPER

Serve in: shot glass

Ᵹ Pour the orange juice, tomato juice, lime juice, and grenadine into
a large mixing bowl.

Ᵹ Add the salt, chili, and Worcestershire sauce plus a couple of grindings
of black pepper and stir well.

Ᵹ Refrigerate for at least 2 hours.

Ᵹ Strain into a pitcher.

Ᵹ Serve both the Sangrita and the tequila in shot glasses, and sip alternately.

What's in a name?

A traditional chaser to drink with neat tequila, the name Sangrita means
"little blood," which is a reference to its red color. It's nonalcoholic but
deliciously spicy: this recipe uses fresh chili but you can use ½ tsp cayenne
pepper for a milder version if you prefer. Drink with reposado tequila if you
can—it has a smoother, more complex flavor than silver tequila, and it
deserves to be drunk neat. This recipe serves six.

Blue Diablo

WEDGE OF LIME
SEA SALT
1 oz TEQUILA
½ oz **LEMON JUICE**
DASH OF LIME CORDIAL
DASH OF BLUE CURAÇAO
Serve in: Old-fashioned glass

℞ Rub the lime wedge over the rim of an Old-fashioned glass.

℞ Dip it in a saucer of finely crushed salt.

℞ Fill a shaker with ice.

℞ Add the tequila, lemon juice, and lime cordial.

℞ Shake.

℞ Strain into the glass filled with ice.

℞ Pour in the blue curaçao. Do not stir.

El Diablo

2 oz TEQUILA
¾ oz **CRÈME DE CASSIS**
¾ oz **LIME JUICE**
GINGER ALE
WEDGE OF LIME
Serve in: highball

℞ Fill a highball with crushed ice.

℞ Add the tequila, crème de cassis, and lime juice.

℞ Stir.

℞ Top off with ginger ale and stir again.

℞ Decorate with the lime wedge.

Blue Diablo

G-Force

1 oz GOLD TEQUILA
1 oz GIN
DASH OF GALLIANO
Serve in: martini glass

℉ Fill a shaker with ice.

℉ Add the tequila, gin, and Galliano.

℉ Shake, then strain into a martini glass.

El Toro

2 oz TEQUILA
1 oz KAHLÚA
1 oz LIGHT CREAM
Serve in: martini glass

℉ Fill a shaker with ice.

℉ Add the tequila, Kahlúa, and cream.

℉ Shake well, so that the cream is mixed in well.

℉ Strain into a martini glass.

Banana Drama

1½ oz TEQUILA
½ oz CRÈME DE BANANE
1 oz LIME JUICE
TWIST OF LIME PEEL
Serve in: martini glass

Y Fill a shaker with ice.

Y Add the tequila, crème de banane, and lime juice.

Y Shake.

Y Strain into a martini glass.

Y Decorate with the lime twist.

High Voltage

2 oz TEQUILA
1 oz PEACH SCHNAPPS
½ oz LIME JUICE
TWIST OF LIME PEEL
Serve in: martini glass

Y Fill a shaker with ice.

Y Add the tequila, Schnapps, and lime juice.

Y Shake.

Y Strain into a martini glass.

Y Decorate with the lime twist.

Silk Stockings

2 oz TEQUILA
1 oz CRÈME DE CACAO
1 oz HEAVY CREAM
DASH OF GRENADINE
Serve in: martini glass

Y Add the tequila, crème de cacao, cream, and grenadine
   to a shaker filled with ice.

Y Shake well, so that the cream mixes in.

Y Strain into a martini glass.

Tequila Mockingbird

1½ oz **TEQUILA**
½ oz **WHITE CRÈME DE MENTHE**
½ oz **LEMON JUICE**
SPRIG OF MINT
SLICE OF LEMON

Serve in: Old-fashioned glass

Ⴘ Fill a shaker with ice.

Ⴘ Pour in the tequila, crème de menthe, and lemon juice.

Ⴘ Shake.

Ⴘ Strain into an Old-fashioned glass filled with crushed ice.

Ⴘ Decorate with the mint sprig and lemon slice.

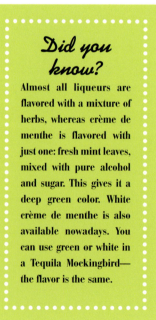

Did you know?

Almost all liqueurs are flavored with a mixture of herbs, whereas crème de menthe is flavored with just one: fresh mint leaves, mixed with pure alcohol and sugar. This gives it a deep green color. White crème de menthe is also available nowadays. You can use green or white in a Tequila Mockingbird— the flavor is the same.

Acapulco

1 oz TEQUILA
1 oz TIA MARIA
1 oz DARK RUM
1 oz PINEAPPLE JUICE
1 oz COCONUT CREAM
PINEAPPLE WEDGE
MARASCHINO CHERRY
Serve in: highball

- Fill a shaker with ice.
- Add all the ingredients except the pineapple wedge and cherry.
- Shake well, so that the coconut cream is fully mixed in.
- Strain into a highball filled with ice.
- Decorate with the pineapple wedge and cherry.

Viva Zapata

1 oz TEQUILA
⅔ oz WHITE CRÈME DE CACAO
⅔ oz MIDORI
1 oz PINEAPPLE JUICE
1 oz ORANGE JUICE
SLICE OF ORANGE
Serve in: highball

- Fill a shaker with ice.
- Pour in the tequila, crème de cacao, and Midori.
- Add the juices.
- Shake.
- Strain into a highball filled with ice.
- Decorate with the orange slice.

Shady Lady

2 oz TEQUILA
1 oz MIDORI
4 oz GRAPEFRUIT JUICE
SLICE OF LIME
Serve in: highball

♈ Fill a highball with crushed ice.

♈ Pour in the tequila, Midori, and grapefruit juice.

♈ Stir.

♈ Decorate with the lime slice.

Sloe Tequila

½ CUP CRUSHED ICE
1 oz TEQUILA
½ oz SLOE GIN
½ oz LIME JUICE
Serve in: martini glass

♈ Put the crushed ice in a blender and add the tequila, sloe gin, and lime juice.

♈ Blend until combined.

♈ Pour into a martini glass.

Rosita

1 oz TEQUILA
½ oz CAMPARI
½ oz DRY VERMOUTH
½ oz SWEET VERMOUTH
TWIST OF ORANGE PEEL

Serve in: Old-fashioned glass

Ῐ Fill an Old-fashioned glass with ice.

Ῐ Add the tequila, Campari, and dry and sweet vermouths.

Ῐ Stir.

Ῐ Drop in the orange twist.

Rude Cosmopolitan

1½ oz TEQUILA
½ oz COINTREAU
1 oz CRANBERRY JUICE
½ oz LIME JUICE
TWIST OF ORANGE PEEL

Serve in: martini glass

Ῐ Fill a shaker with ice.

Ῐ Add all the ingredients except the orange twist.

Ῐ Shake.

Ῐ Strain into a martini glass.

Ῐ Decorate with the orange twist.

RUM

Rum is made from molasses, a by-product of sugar cane. This cash crop was introduced to the Caribbean by Christopher Columbus—who in fact landed there in 1492 and not on the North American continent. Rum became the national drink in the 17th century, and was adopted by Britain's Royal Navy as a cheap tipple for sailors. The associations remain, both with the Caribbean islands and with English seamen.

Each Caribbean island group has developed its own style of rum, and there are some specialty producers who make premium rum from pressed sugar cane rather than molasses. Regional specialties apart, there are three main types of rum: white, gold, and dark. The difference between them depends on the length of time the spirit is aged in its oak barrels.

White rum is aged for less than a year, and is light-bodied with a subtle flavor. It makes an excellent base for cocktails, and goes particularly well with fruit juices, coconut, chocolate liqueur, and cola. Gold rum is aged for several years, and is smoother and slightly sweeter than white rum. The dark rums—which are aged for anything up to thirty years—have a full body and rich, caramel flavors. All rums are used in cocktails—and sometimes all three types are combined in one drink—but the premium dark rums are as fine as an excellent malt whiskey or a good Cognac, and should be enjoyed neat.

Rum Sour

2 oz GOLD OR DARK RUM
1 oz LIME JUICE
1 TSP SUPERFINE SUGAR
Serve in: Old-fashioned glass

℆ Fill a shaker with ice.

℆ Pour in the rum and lime juice.

℆ Add the sugar.

℆ Shake until the sugar has dissolved.

℆ Pour into an Old-fashioned glass.

Rum Gimlet

2 oz WHITE RUM
1 oz LIME CORDIAL
SLICE OF LIME
Serve in: Old-fashioned glass

℆ Fill an Old-fashioned glass with ice.

℆ Pour in the rum and cordial.

℆ Stir.

℆ Drop in the lime slice.

Pink Rum

2 oz GOLD RUM
1 oz LIME JUICE
½ TSP GRENADINE
1 TSP SUPERFINE SUGAR
Serve in: martini glass

℆ Fill a shaker with ice.

℆ Add the rum, lime juice, grenadine, and sugar.

℆ Shake well.

℆ Strain into a martini glass.

Pale Pink Rum

2 oz GOLD RUM
1 oz GIN
1 oz LIME JUICE
½ TSP GRENADINE
1 TSP SUPERFINE SUGAR
Serve in: martini glass

Y Fill a shaker with ice.

Y Pour in the rum, gin, lime juice, grenadine, and sugar.

Y Shake well.

Y Strain into a martini glass.

Rum Daisy

2 oz WHITE RUM
1 oz LEMON JUICE
1 oz ORANGE JUICE
1 TSP GRENADINE
SLICE OF ORANGE
Serve in: Old-fashioned glass

Y Fill a shaker with ice.

Y Add the gin, juices, and grenadine.

Y Shake.

Y Strain into an Old-fashioned glass.

Y Decorate with the orange slice.

Caribbean Breeze

1½ oz **DARK RUM**
1 oz **CRÈME DE BANANE**
3 oz **PINEAPPLE JUICE**
2 oz **CRANBERRY JUICE**
½ oz **LIME JUICE**
WEDGE OF LIME
SLICE OF PINEAPPLE
Serve in: goblet

Ⴤ Fill a shaker with ice.

Ⴤ Add the rum, crème de banane, and the juices.

Ⴤ Strain into a goblet over crushed ice.

Ⴤ Decorate with the lime wedge, pineapple slice and leaf (optional).

Scorpion

1 oz **DARK RUM**
½ oz **WHITE RUM**
½ oz **BRANDY**
½ oz **COINTREAU**
2 oz **ORANGE JUICE**
1 oz **LIME JUICE**
½ oz **ORGEAT**
WEDGE OF LIME
Serve in: highball

Bartender's tip
If you can't find Orgeat syrup, use Amaretto or leave it out altogether.

Ⴤ Fill a shaker with ice.

Ⴤ Pour in the rums, brandy, Cointreau, juices, and syrup.

Ⴤ Shake.

Ⴤ Strain into a highball filled with ice.

Ⴤ Decorate with the lime wedge.

Caribbean Breeze

Bacardi Cocktail

1½ oz **BACARDI**
½ oz **LIME JUICE**
¼ oz **GRENADINE**
SLICE OF LIME
Serve in: cocktail glass

ᵀ Fill a shaker with ice.

ᵀ Add the Bacardi, lime juice,
   and grenadine and shake.

ᵀ Strain into a cocktail glass.

ᵀ Decorate with the lime slice.

Did you know?

This cocktail was created by Bacardi in the early 1900s. In 1936, the company sued a restaurant that made the drink with another rum and eventually won a U.S. ruling that anyone selling a Bacardi Cocktail must make it with Bacardi.

• •

Bacardi Special

1½ oz **BACARDI**
1 oz **GIN**
½ oz **LIME JUICE**
¼ oz **GRENADINE**
SLICE OF LIME
Serve in: cocktail glass

ᵀ Fill a shaker with ice.

ᵀ Pour in the Bacardi, gin, lime juice, and grenadine.

ᵀ Shake, then strain into a cocktail glass.

ᵀ Drop in the lime slice.

• •

Poker

2 oz **WHITE RUM**
1 oz **SWEET VERMOUTH**
TWIST OF ORANGE PEEL
Serve in: martini glass

ᵀ Fill a shaker with ice.

ᵀ Add the rum and vermouth.

ᵀ Strain into a martini glass.

ᵀ Drop in the orange twist.

Statue of Liberty

1 oz WHITE RUM
1 oz CALVADOS OR APPLEJACK
1 TSP SUPERFINE SUGAR
SLICE OF LEMON
Serve in: cocktail glass

℈ Fill a shaker with ice.

℈ Add the rum, Calvados or applejack, and sugar.

℈ Shake well, then strain into the glass.

℈ Decorate with the lemon slice.

XYZ

2 oz DARK RUM
1 oz COINTREAU
1 oz LEMON JUICE
TWIST OF LEMON PEEL
Serve in: martini glass

℈ Fill a shaker with ice.

℈ Add the rum, Cointreau, and lemon juice.

℈ Shake.

℈ Strain into a martini glass.

℈ Decorate with the lemon twist.

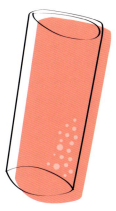

Cuba Libre

2 oz WHITE RUM
1 oz LIME JUICE
COLA
SLICE OF LIME
Serve in: highball

Y Fill a highball with ice.

Y Add the rum and lime juice.

Y Stir.

Y Top off with cola and stir again.

Y Decorate with the lime slice.

Did you know?

This cocktail was created in 1893 when an inventive soldier based in Cuba mixed local rum with a new tonic beverage—Coca Cola.

Dark and Stormy

2 oz DARK RUM
½ oz LIME JUICE
GINGER BEER OR ALE
WEDGE OF LIME
Serve in: highball

Y Fill a highball with ice.

Y Add the rum and lime juice.

Y Top off with ginger beer or ale.

Y Stir again.

Y Decorate with the lime wedge.

Hurricane

1 oz WHITE RUM
1 oz DARK RUM
1 oz LIME JUICE
1 oz PINEAPPLE JUICE
1 oz ORANGE JUICE
½ oz BLACK CURRANT SYRUP
SLICE OF PINEAPPLE
MARASCHINO CHERRY
Serve in: highball or goblet

Y Fill a shaker with ice.

Y Add the rums, juices, and syrup.

Y Strain into a highball or goblet.

Y Decorate with the pineapple slice and

  the cherry.

Rum Cooler

1½ oz WHITE RUM
½ oz COINTREAU
2 oz ORANGE JUICE
½ oz LIME JUICE
DASH OF GRENADINE
LEMONADE
TWIST OF ORANGE PEEL
Serve in: highball

Y Fill a shaker with ice.

Y Add the rum, Cointreau, orange juice, lime juice, and grenadine.

Y Shake.

Y Strain into a highball filled with ice.

Y Top off with lemonade.

Y Decorate with the orange twist.

Christopher Columbus

1½ oz GOLD RUM
1 oz APRICOT BRANDY
1 oz PINEAPPLE JUICE
½ oz LIME JUICE
SLICE OF LIME
WEDGE OF PINEAPPLE
Serve in: Old-fashioned glass

♈ Fill a shaker with ice.

♈ Pour in the rum, apricot brandy, and juices and shake.

♈ Strain into an Old-fashioned glass filled with ice.

♈ Decorate with the lime slice and pineapple wedge.

El Burro

½ CUP CRUSHED ICE
½ oz DARK RUM
½ oz KAHLÚA
1 oz COCONUT CREAM
1 oz LIGHT CREAM
½ BANANA, SLICED
SPRIG OF MINT
Serve in: Old-fashioned glass

♈ Add the ice to a blender.

♈ Pour in the dark rum, Kahlúa, coconut cream, cream, and the sliced banana.

♈ Blend until smooth.

♈ Pour into an Old-fashioned glass.

♈ Decorate with the mint sprig.

Golden Beach

2 oz GOLD RUM
½ oz BROWN CRÈME DE CACAO
1 oz LIME JUICE
SLICE OF LIME
Serve in: martini glass

♈ Fill a shaker with ice.

♈ Pour in the rum, crème de cacao, and lime juice.

♈ Strain into a martini glass.

♈ Decorate with the lime slice.

La Floridita

1½ oz WHITE RUM
½ oz LIME JUICE
½ oz SWEET VERMOUTH
½ oz CRÈME DE CACAO
1 TSP GRENADINE
TWIST OF LIME PEEL
Serve in: martini glass

Ⓨ Fill a shaker with ice.

Ⓨ Add all the ingredients except the lime twist.

Ⓨ Shake well.

Ⓨ Strain into a martini glass.

Ⓨ Decorate with the lime twist.

Love in the Afternoon

1 CUP CRUSHED ICE
1 oz DARK RUM
½ oz CRÈME DE FRAISE
1 oz FRESH ORANGE JUICE
1 oz COCONUT CREAM
½ oz SUGAR SYRUP (SEE PAGE 19)
½ oz LIGHT CREAM
3–4 STRAWBERRIES, PLUS EXTRA SLICE
Serve in: goblet

Ⓨ Put the crushed ice in a blender.

Ⓨ Pour in the rum, crème de fraise, orange juice, coconut cream, sugar syrup, and cream.

Ⓨ Add the strawberries.

Ⓨ Blend until smooth.

Ⓨ Pour into a goblet.

Ⓨ Decorate with the extra strawberry slice.

Mojito

1 TSP SUPERFINE SUGAR
1 oz LIME JUICE
8–10 MINT LEAVES
2 oz GOLD OR DARK RUM
DASH OF SPARKLING WATER

Serve in: Old-fashioned glass

Y Put the sugar and lime juice into an Old-fashioned glass.

Y Add the mint leaves.

Y Muddle or crush with the back of a spoon.

Y Pour in the rum.

Y Add 4 or 5 ice cubes.

Y Top off with sparkling water.

Did you know?

The Mojito is a traditional Cuban drink that's been around since at least the 1930s. The writer Ernest Hemingway was one famous aficionado: he used to enjoy them at the Bodeguita restaurant in Havana, which is still going strong. The Mojito was originally made with white rum, but using gold or dark rum gives a much better flavor. Some people also like to add a couple of drops of Angostura bitters to the rum.

Planter's Punch

2 oz WHITE RUM
1 oz DARK RUM
½ oz COINTREAU
1 oz LEMON JUICE
1 oz ORANGE JUICE
½ oz PINEAPPLE JUICE
DASH OF GRENADINE
SLICE OF ORANGE
SLICE OF LEMON
SLICE OF PINEAPPLE

Serve in: highball

Bartender's tip
This is a good party cocktail: increase the quantity and make in a pitcher.

Ⓨ Fill a shaker with ice.

Ⓨ Add the rums, Cointreau, juices, and grenadine.

Ⓨ Shake.

Ⓨ Strain into a highball filled with ice.

Ⓨ Decorate with orange, lemon, and pineapple slices.

Yellow Bird

1 oz **WHITE RUM**
½ oz **CRÈME DE BANANE**
½ oz **GALLIANO**
½ oz **LIME JUICE**
½ oz **PINEAPPLE JUICE**
TWIST OF LIME PEEL
Serve in: martini glass

Y Fill a shaker with ice.

Y Add the rum, crème de banane, Galliano, lime juice, and pineapple juice.

Y Shake.

Y Strain into a martini glass.

Y Decorate with the lime twist.

Liquid Banana

1½ oz **DARK RUM**
¾ oz **CRÈME DE BANANE**
2 oz **LEMON JUICE**
SLICE OF LEMON
Serve in: martini glass

Y Fill a shaker with ice.

Y Pour in the rum and crème de banane.

Y Add the lemon juice.

Y Shake.

Y Strain into a martini glass.

Y Decorate with the lemon slice.

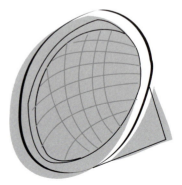

Hot Buttered Rum

1 TSP BROWN SUGAR
PIECE OF UNSALTED BUTTER
1 TSP GROUND CINNAMON
2 oz DARK RUM
Serve in: heatproof goblet

Bartender's tip
To prevent cracking,
use heatproof glasses,
or stand a spoon in
them before adding
hot liquid.

Y Place the sugar in the goblet
and add a little hot water.
Stir until the sugar has
partly dissolved.

Y Add the butter and cinnamon.
Stir again.

Y Pour in the rum.

Y Top off with hot water.

Y Stir well to dissolve the sugar
and melt the butter.

Blue Waters

1 oz WHITE RUM
½ oz COINTREAU
½ oz BLUE CURAÇAO
1 oz LIME JUICE
2 oz PINEAPPLE JUICE
WEDGE OF PINEAPPLE
Serve in: highball

Y Fill a shaker with ice.

Y Add the rum, Cointreau, blue curaçao, and juices.

Y Shake, then strain into a highball filled with ice.

Y Decorate with the pineapple wedge.

WHISKEY

You could spend a lifetime exploring the subtle varieties of whiskey. There is Scotch, Irish whiskey, bourbon, rye, and Canadian whisky. Then there are all the variants on these: there are hundreds of Scotch single malts to choose from alone.

All whiskey is made from grain: barley, corn, rye, and wheat. The taste depends on which grains are used in what proportion, and whether they are malted first. Scotch malts are generally considered to be the finest. They are made entirely from barley, and are aged for at least eight years. A blended Scotch is produced by combining single malts and adding two or three grain whiskeys, a process that leads to a smooth, consistent flavor. Scotch malts should be drunk alone, or with a dash of water, but blended Scotch goes well in cocktails.

American bourbon originated in Kentucky more than 200 years ago. By law it has to be made with at least 50 percent corn and must be aged in burnt oak, which helps develop its sweetness. It is used in a variety of cocktails, including the Mint Julep and the Sazerac.

Canadian whisky is often dubbed rye, but is usually a smooth blend of different grains. True rye whiskey usually comes from the United States: it contains more than 50 percent rye, which gives it a distinctive flavor. Irish whiskey is similar to Scotch, but slightly sweeter.

Hot Toddy

2 oz SCOTCH WHISKY
1 TSP HONEY
HOT WATER
CINNAMON STICK
SLICE OF LEMON
Serve in: heatproof goblet

Y Pour the Scotch into a heatproof goblet.

Y Add the honey.

Y Stir.

Y Pour in the hot water.

Y Stir again to dissolve the honey.

Y Drop in the cinnamon stick and lemon slice.

Cold Toddy

½ TSP SUGAR
1 TSP HOT WATER
2 oz SCOTCH WHISKY
SLICE OF LEMON
Serve in: Old-fashioned glass

Y Put the sugar in an Old-fashioned glass.

Y Add the water, and stir to dissolve.

Y Add 2 or 3 ice cubes.

Y Pour in the whisky and stir.

Y Drop in the lemon slice.

Whisky Mac

1 oz SCOTCH WHISKY
1 oz GREEN GINGER WINE
Serve in: Old-fashioned glass

Y Fill an Old-fashioned glass with ice.

Y Pour in the whisky.

Y Add the green ginger wine.

Y Stir.

Whiskey Sour

2 oz **WHISKEY OF CHOICE**
1 oz **LEMON JUICE**
DASH OF ANGOSTURA BITTERS
1 TSP **SUGAR (OPTIONAL)**
TWIST OF LEMON PEEL
Serve in: sour glass

Ϋ Fill a shaker with ice.

Ϋ Add the whiskey, lemon juice, bitters, and sugar, if using.

Ϋ Shake, then strain into a sour glass.

Ϋ Decorate with the lemon twist.

Whisky and French

1 oz **VERMOUTH**
2 oz **SCOTCH WHISKY**
Serve in: sherry glass

Ϋ Pour the vermouth into a sherry glass.

Ϋ Add the whisky.

Ϋ Stir.

Canadian Whisky Cocktail

2 oz **CANADIAN WHISKY**
½ oz **COINTREAU**
DASH OF ORANGE BITTERS
1 TSP **SUPERFINE SUGAR**
TWIST OF LEMON PEEL
Serve in: martini glass

Ϋ Fill a shaker with ice.

Ϋ Add the whisky, Cointreau, bitters, and sugar.

Ϋ Shake well.

Ϋ Strain into a martini glass.

Ϋ Drop in the lemon twist.

Kentucky Blizzard

2 oz BOURBON
1 oz CRANBERRY JUICE
½ oz LIME JUICE
DASH OF GRENADINE
1 TSP SUPERFINE SUGAR
SLICE OF LEMON
2–3 CRANBERRIES
Serve in: highball

Y Fill a shaker with ice.

Y Add the bourbon, cranberry juice, lime juice, grenadine, and sugar.

Y Shake well.

Y Strain into a highball filled with ice.

Y Decorate with the lemon slice and cranberries.

Whiskey Daisy

2 oz BOURBON
1 oz LEMON JUICE
DASH OF GRENADINE
CLUB SODA
SLICE OF LEMON
Serve in: highball

Y Fill a shaker with ice.

Y Add the bourbon, lemon juice, and grenadine.

Y Shake.

Y Strain into a highball filled with ice.

Y Top off with club soda.

Y Stir, then decorate with the lemon slice.

Whiskey Cooler

2 oz BOURBON
1 oz LIME JUICE
1 TSP SUPERFINE SUGAR
GINGER ALE
TWIST OF LIME PEEL
Serve in: highball

- ♈ Fill a shaker with ice.
- ♈ Add the bourbon, lime juice, and sugar.
- ♈ Shake well.
- ♈ Strain into a highball filled with ice.
- ♈ Top off with ginger ale.
- ♈ Decorate with the lime twist.

• •

California Lemonade

2 oz WHISKEY OF CHOICE
1 oz LEMON JUICE
½ oz LIME JUICE
½ TSP GRENADINE
1 TSP SUPERFINE SUGAR
CLUB SODA
SLICE OF LIME
SLICE OF LEMON
MARASCHINO CHERRY
Serve in: highball

- ♈ Fill a shaker with ice.
- ♈ Add the whiskey, lemon and lime juices, grenadine, and sugar.
- ♈ Shake well.
- ♈ Strain into a highball filled with ice.
- ♈ Top off with club soda.
- ♈ Decorate with the lemon and lime slices and the cherry.

Algonquin

2 oz RYE WHISKEY
1 oz DRY VERMOUTH
1 oz PINEAPPLE JUICE
SLICE OF LEMON
Serve in: Old-fashioned glass

♈ Fill a shaker with ice.

♈ Add the rye, vermouth, and pineapple juice.

♈ Shake.

♈ Strain into an Old-fashioned glass half-filled with ice.

♈ Decorate with the lemon slice.

Pamplemousse

1 oz CANADIAN WHISKY
1 oz SOUTHERN COMFORT
2 oz GRAPEFRUIT JUICE
1 oz PINEAPPLE SYRUP
   (FROM A CAN OF FRUIT)
WEDGE OF PINEAPPLE
MARASCHINO CHERRY
Serve in: Old-fashioned glass

What's in a name?

"Pamplemousse" is the amusing French word for "grapefruit," which is how this drink got its name.

♈ Fill a shaker with ice.

♈ Add the whisky, Southern Comfort, grapefruit juice, and pineapple syrup.

♈ Shake.

♈ Strain into an Old-fashioned glass.

♈ Decorate with the pineapple wedge and cherry.

Whisky Fancy
2 oz CANADIAN WHISKY
1 oz COINTREAU
SLICE OF LEMON
Serve in: martini glass

☙ Fill a shaker with ice.

☙ Add the whisky and Cointreau.

☙ Shake.

☙ Strain into a martini glass.

☙ Decorate with the lemon slice.

Aquarius
2 oz SCOTCH WHISKY
1 oz CHERRY BRANDY
2 oz CRANBERRY JUICE
1 TSP SUPERFINE SUGAR
MARASCHINO CHERRY
Serve in: Old-fashioned glass

☙ Add the Scotch, cherry brandy, cranberry juice, and sugar to a shaker filled with ice.

☙ Shake well.

☙ Strain into an Old-fashioned glass.

☙ Decorate with the cherry.

Millionaire

2 oz WHISKEY OF CHOICE
⅔ oz COINTREAU
DASH OF GRENADINE
DASH OF CRÈME DE FRAMBOISE
½ AN EGG WHITE
WEDGE OF LEMON
Serve in: martini glass

Ⓨ Fill a shaker with ice.

Ⓨ Add the whiskey, Cointreau, grenadine, crème de framboise, and egg white.

Ⓨ Shake well, so that the egg white is thoroughly mixed in.

Ⓨ Strain into a martini glass.

Ⓨ Decorate with the lemon wedge.

New Yorker

2 oz BOURBON
1 oz LEMON JUICE
1 TSP SUPERFINE SUGAR
½ TSP GRENADINE
TWIST OF LEMON PEEL
Serve in: martini glass

Ⓨ Fill a shaker with ice.

Ⓨ Add the bourbon, lemon juice, sugar, and grenadine.

Ⓨ Shake.

Ⓨ Strain into a martini glass.

Ⓨ Decorate with the lemon twist.

Godfather

2 oz WHISKEY OF CHOICE
1 oz AMARETTO
Serve in: Old-fashioned glass

Ⓨ Fill an Old-fashioned glass with ice.

Ⓨ Pour in the whiskey.

Ⓨ Add the Amaretto.

Ⓨ Stir lightly.

Millionaire

Dixie Dew

2 oz BOURBON
½ TSP WHITE CRÈME DE MENTHE
½ TSP COINTREAU
Serve in: martini glass

Y Fill a shaker with ice.

Y Add the bourbon, crème de menthe, and Cointreau.

Y Shake.

Y Strain into a glass.

Rusty Nail

2 oz SCOTCH WHISKY
1 oz DRAMBUIE
TWIST OF LEMON PEEL
Serve in: Old-fashioned glass

Y Add 2 or 3 ice cubes to an
  Old-fashioned glass.

Y Pour in the Scotch.

Y Add the Drambuie and stir.

Y Drop in the lemon twist.

Did you know?

This is an excellent cocktail for after dinner. And it is easy to make, too, since it is simply mixed in the glass.

Commodore

1½ oz SCOTCH WHISKY OR BOURBON
½ oz LIME JUICE
1 TSP SUGAR SYRUP (SEE PAGE 19)
DASH OF ORANGE BITTERS
SLICE OF ORANGE
Serve in: martini glass

Y Fill a shaker with ice.

Y Add the Scotch or bourbon, lime juice, sugar syrup, and bitters.

Y Shake.

Y Strain into a martini glass.

Y Decorate with the orange slice.

Blood and Sand

1 oz SCOTCH WHISKY
½ oz CHERRY BRANDY
½ oz SWEET VERMOUTH
1 oz ORANGE JUICE
SLICE OF ORANGE
Serve in: martini glass

♈ Shake the Scotch, cherry brandy, vermouth, and orange juice over ice.

♈ Strain into a martini glass.

♈ Decorate with the orange slice.

Frisco

2 oz RYE WHISKEY
½ oz BENEDICTINE
¾ oz LEMON JUICE
SLICE OF LEMON
Serve in: martini glass

♈ Fill a shaker with ice.

♈ Add the rye, Benedictine, and lemon juice.

♈ Shake, then strain into a martini glass.

♈ Decorate with the lemon slice.

Did you know?

Pure gold—this one has been around since the California Gold Rush. Traditionally, rye is used but you can make this cocktail with bourbon if you prefer it. You can also add a teaspoon of superfine sugar to sweeten the mix.

Sazerac

1 SUGAR LUMP
1 TSP PERNOD
2 DASHES PEYCHAUD'S OR ANGOSTURA BITTERS
2 oz BOURBON OR RYE WHISKEY
TWIST OF LEMON PEEL
Serve in: Old-fashioned glass

- Place the sugar lump in the bottom of an Old-fashioned glass.
- Soak with the Pernod and bitters.
- Crush the soaked sugar lump using a muddler or the back of a spoon.
- Add 3 or 4 ice cubes to the glass.
- Pour in the bourbon.
- Stir.
- Decorate with the lemon twist.

What's in a name?

For a really authentic Sazerac, it has to be Peychaud's bitters. Its creator—Frenchman Antoine Peychaud—came up with the recipe in the early 18th century, and sold the concoction at his drugstore in New Orleans. The Sazerac was one of the world's first cocktails—and some people say that the name "cocktail" comes from a mispronunciation of the French word for eggcup, which is what Peychaud used to serve his drink in.

Benedict

2 oz SCOTCH WHISKY
1 oz BENEDICTINE
GINGER ALE
Serve in: highball

- Fill a mixing glass with ice.
- Add the Scotch and Benedictine.
- Stir.
- Pour into a highball (do not strain).
- Top off with ginger ale.

Sazerac

Tipperary
2 oz IRISH WHISKEY
½ oz GREEN CHARTREUSE
½ oz SWEET VERMOUTH
MARASCHINO CHERRY
Serve in: martini glass

- Fill a shaker with ice.
- Add the whiskey, Chartreuse, and sweet vermouth.
- Shake.
- Strain into a martini glass.
- Decorate with the cherry.

Apple Snap
¾ oz BOURBON
¾ oz APPLE SCHNAPPS
¼ TSP GROUND CINNAMON
Serve in: Old-fashioned glass

- Pour the bourbon into an Old-fashioned glass filled with ice.
- Add the Schnapps; do not stir.
- Sprinkle the cinnamon over the top.

Whiskey Milk Punch

2 oz BOURBON
1 TSP SUPERFINE SUGAR
4 oz MILK
¼ TSP GROUND NUTMEG
Serve in: Old-fashioned glass

Ⓨ Fill a shaker with ice.

Ⓨ Add the bourbon, sugar, and milk.

Ⓨ Shake well.

Ⓨ Pour into an Old-fashioned glass.

Ⓨ Sprinkle the nutmeg over the top.

Bartender's tip
You can use cinnamon instead of the nutmeg if you prefer it.

Allegheny

1 oz BOURBON
1 oz DRY VERMOUTH
2 TSP CRÈME DE MÛRE
2 TSP LEMON JUICE
1 WHOLE BLACKBERRY
Serve in: martini glass

Ⓨ Fill a shaker with ice.

Ⓨ Pour in the bourbon, vermouth, crème de mûre, and lemon juice.

Ⓨ Shake, then strain into a martini glass.

Ⓨ Drop in the blackberry to decorate.

BRANDY

The word "brandy" comes from the Dutch *brandewijn*, which means "burnt wine." The term came about when traders from the Netherlands took to boiling down cheap French wine over a fire so that it did not take up so much room on their ships—or incur so much duty. The idea was to add water once the cargo was unloaded, but they found that some wines benefited from the reduction process. The wine that tasted best after boiling came from a little town near La Rochelle by the name of Cognac.

In modern times, Cognac is always blended, and by law has to be aged for at least two and a half years; the finest Cognacs are aged for decades. Cognac has a rounded flavor, which means it works well in cocktails, but don't use the finest blends—these deserve to be drunk on their own.

Although Cognac is considered the most perfect form of brandy, some connoisseurs prefer Armagnac, produced in Gascony, France. Unlike Cognac, Armagnac is not always blended: you can buy single-estate or single-vintage Armagnac.

Other good brandies come from Spain. The best are produced by the sherry houses of Jerez. Brandy is produced by the Cognac method in California and—surprisingly—in the former Soviet state of Armenia. Winston Churchill— a man who knew his brandy—preferred Armenian Cognac to the French original.

Cognac producers use the following terms: VS (very special, at least three years old); VSOP (very special old pale, at least five years old); XO (extra old, at least six years old). Old brandies may also be termed Grande Réserve, Extra Vieille, or Napoléon. Armagnac is labeled in a similar way.

Brandy Crusta

WEDGE OF ORANGE
SUPERFINE SUGAR
1 oz BRANDY
½ oz LIQUID FROM A JAR OF MARASCHINO CHERRIES
1 oz ORANGE JUICE
DASH OF ANGOSTURA BITTERS
SLICE OF ORANGE
Serve in: champagne flute

- Rub the orange wedge over the rim of a champagne flute.
- Dip in a saucer of the sugar.
- Fill a shaker with ice.
- Add the brandy, maraschino juice, orange juice, and bitters.
- Shake.
- Strain into the flute.
- Decorate with a slice of orange.

• •

Brandy Daisy

2 oz BRANDY
1 oz LEMON JUICE
1 TSP GRENADINE
½ TSP SUPERFINE SUGAR
MARASCHINO CHERRY
Serve in: Old-fashioned glass

- Place the brandy, lemon juice, grenadine, and sugar in a shaker filled with ice.
- Shake well.
- Strain into an Old-fashioned glass.
- Drop in the cherry to decorate.

Brandy Crusta

Brandy Alexander

1 oz BRANDY
1 oz BROWN CRÈME DE CACAO
1 oz HEAVY CREAM
WHOLE OR GROUND NUTMEG
Serve in: martini glass

Ⅲ Half-fill a shaker with ice.

Ⅲ Add the brandy, crème de cacao, and cream.

Ⅲ Shake well.

Ⅲ Strain into a martini glass.

Ⅲ Grate a little fresh nutmeg (or sprinkle ground nutmeg)
   over the top to decorate.

Bartender's tip
Try grated semisweet chocolate in place of the nutmeg.

Did you know?

This heavenly concoction is a superb after-dinner cocktail – it is practically a dessert in itself. But it also makes an excellent first drink at a cocktail party, not least because the cream will help line your stomach. The traditional recipe uses brown crème de cacao (chocolate liqueur) but you can also make a White Alexander using white crème de cacao. Delicious.

Brandy Sour

2 oz **BRANDY**
1 oz **LEMON JUICE**
½ **TSP SUPERFINE SUGAR**
MARASCHINO CHERRY
SLICE OF ORANGE

Serve in: Old-fashioned glass

Ⓨ Place the brandy, lemon juice, and sugar in a shaker filled with ice.

Ⓨ Shake well.

Ⓨ Strain into an Old-fashioned glass.

Ⓨ Decorate with the cherry and orange slice.

....

B and B

½ oz **BENEDICTINE**
½ oz **BRANDY**

Serve in: brandy glass

Ⓨ Pour the Benedictine into an unchilled brandy glass.

Ⓨ Pour in the brandy; do not stir.

Ⓨ Swirl the glass in your hand, to warm the brandy and release its aromas.

....

Brandy Mac

1 **TSP SUPERFINE SUGAR**
DASH OF HOT WATER
1 oz **BRANDY**
1 oz **GREEN GINGER WINE**

Serve in: Old-fashioned glass

Ⓨ Put the sugar in the bottom of an Old-fashioned glass.

Ⓨ Add the hot water and stir to dissolve the sugar.

Ⓨ Pour in the brandy and green ginger wine.

Ⓨ Stir.

Hot tip
A variation of that famous cure for colds, the Whisky Mac (*see page 138*), this one is just as warming and tastes equally good.

Brandy Buster

1 oz BRANDY
½ oz DRY VERMOUTH
½ oz LIME JUICE
GINGER ALE
SLICE OF LEMON
Serve in: highball

Ỹ Fill a shaker with ice.

Ỹ Pour in the brandy, vermouth, and lime juice.

Ỹ Stir, then strain into a highball filled with ice.

Ỹ Top off with the ginger ale.

Ỹ Stir again.

Ỹ Decorate with the lemon slice.

• •

Brandy Highball

1 oz BRANDY
DASH OF ANGOSTURA BITTERS
GINGER ALE
TWIST OF LEMON PEEL
Serve in: highball

Ỹ Fill a highball with ice.

Ỹ Pour in the brandy and bitters.

Ỹ Stir.

Ỹ Top off with ginger ale.

Ỹ Stir again.

Ỹ Decorate with the lemon twist.

Brandy Buster

Lancer Franc

1½ oz BRANDY
¾ oz CRÈME DE FRAISE
ORANGE JUICE
SLICE OF ORANGE
Serve in: highball

℞ Fill a highball with ice.

℞ Pour in the brandy and crème de fraise.

℞ Top off with orange juice.

℞ Decorate with the orange slice.

Brandy Sangaree

½ TSP SUPERFINE SUGAR
1 TSP HOT WATER
2 oz BRANDY
CLUB SODA
½ oz PORT
WHOLE OR GROUND NUTMEG
Serve in: highball

℞ Put the superfine sugar in a mixing glass.

℞ Add the water and stir to dissolve.

℞ Pour in the brandy.

℞ Stir again.

℞ Pour into a highball filled with ice.

℞ Top off with club soda.

℞ Add the port, pouring it over the back of a spoon so that it floats on the top of the drink.

℞ Grate a little fresh nutmeg (or sprinkle ground nutmeg) over the top to decorate.

Brandy Horse's Neck

PEEL OF 1 LEMON, CUT IN A SPIRAL (SEE PAGE 74)
2 oz BRANDY
½ oz LEMON JUICE
GINGER ALE
Serve in: highball

- ♟ Hang the lemon spiral over the edge of the highball, so that most of it is inside the glass.
- ♟ Fill the glass with ice.
- ♟ Add the brandy and lemon juice.
- ♟ Stir.
- ♟ Top off with the ginger ale.
- ♟ Stir again.

Egg Nog

1 CUP OF CRUSHED ICE
1 oz BRANDY
1 oz DARK RUM
1 EGG
3 oz MILK
1 TBSP SUGAR SYRUP (SEE PAGE 19)
WHOLE OR GROUND NUTMEG
Serve in: highball

- ♟ Put the crushed ice in a blender.
- ♟ Add the brandy, rum, egg, milk, and sugar syrup.
- ♟ Blend until thoroughly mixed.
- ♟ Pour into a highball (do not strain).
- ♟ Grate a little fresh nutmeg (or sprinkle ground nutmeg) over the top to decorate.

Kiss on the Lips

1½ oz BRANDY
½ oz COINTREAU
½ oz CRÈME DE FRAMBOISE
1 FRESH RASPBERRY
Serve in: martini glass

Y Fill a shaker with ice.

Y Add the brandy, Cointreau, and crème de framboise.

Y Shake.

Y Strain into a martini glass.

Y Drop in the raspberry to decorate.

Corpse Reviver

1 oz BRANDY
½ oz CALVADOS OR APPLEJACK
½ oz SWEET VERMOUTH
Serve in: martini glass

Y Fill a shaker with ice.

Y Pour in the brandy, Calvados or applejack, and sweet vermouth.

Y Shake.

Y Strain into a martini glass.

Did you know?

This 1920s classic is widely held to be a pick-me-up for the morning after, hence its ghoulish name.

Brandy Cassis

1½ oz **BRANDY**
½ oz **CRÈME DE CASSIS**
½ oz **LEMON JUICE**
TWIST OF LEMON PEEL
Serve in: martini glass

Y Fill a shaker with ice.

Y Add the brandy, crème de cassis, and lemon juice.

Y Shake.

Y Strain into a martini glass.

Y Decorate with the lemon twist.

Morning Glory

1 oz **BRANDY**
½ oz **ORANGE CURAÇAO**
½ oz **LEMON JUICE**
DASH OF ANGOSTURA BITTERS
DASH OF PERNOD
TWIST OF LEMON PEEL
Serve in: martini glass

Y Fill a shaker with ice.

Y Add the brandy, orange curaçao, lemon juice, bitters, and Pernod.

Y Shake.

Y Strain into a martini glass.

Y Decorate with the lemon twist.

American Beauty

½ oz **BRANDY**
½ oz **DRY VERMOUTH**
½ oz **ORANGE JUICE**
½ oz **PORT**
1 TSP WHITE CRÈME DE MENTHE
1 TSP GRENADINE
Serve in: martini glass

Ψ Fill a shaker with ice.

Ψ Pour in the brandy, vermouth, orange juice, and port.

Ψ Add the crème de menthe and grenadine.

Ψ Shake.

Ψ Strain into a martini glass.

• •

Cherry Blossom

2 oz **BRANDY**
½ oz **CHERRY BRANDY**
½ oz **COINTREAU**
½ oz **LEMON JUICE**
1 TSP GRENADINE
MARASCHINO CHERRY
Serve in: martini glass

Ψ Fill a shaker with ice.

Ψ Add the brandy, cherry brandy, Cointreau, lemon juice, and grenadine.

Ψ Shake.

Ψ Strain into a martini glass.

Ψ Decorate with the cherry.

Parisien

2 oz BRANDY
1 oz DRY VERMOUTH
DASH OF PERNOD
Serve in: martini glass

♟ Fill a shaker with ice.

♟ Pour in the brandy and vermouth.

♟ Add the Pernod, and shake.

♟ Strain into a martini glass.

••

Bonnie Prince Charlie

1 oz BRANDY
½ oz DRAMBUIE
1 TSP LEMON JUICE
TWIST OF LEMON PEEL
Serve in: martini glass

♟ Shake the brandy, Drambuie, and lemon juice in an ice-filled shaker.

♟ Strain into a martini glass.

♟ Drop in the lemon twist.

••

Chocolate Soldier

1 oz BRANDY
1 oz DRY VERMOUTH
1 oz CRÈME DE CACAO
DASH OF ORANGE BITTERS
TWIST OF ORANGE PEEL
Serve in: martini glass

♟ Fill a shaker with ice.

♟ Pour in the brandy, dry vermouth, and crème de cacao.

♟ Add the orange bitters.

♟ Shake.

♟ Strain into a martini glass.

♟ Decorate with the orange twist.

TNT

1 oz BRANDY
½ oz ORANGE CURAÇAO
DASH OF ORANGE BITTERS
DASH OF PERNOD
SLICE OF ORANGE
Serve in: martini glass

Ⓨ Add all the ingredients except the slice of orange to a mixing glass filled with ice.

Ⓨ Stir.

Ⓨ Strain into a martini glass.

Ⓨ Decorate with the orange slice.

Vanderbilt

1½ oz BRANDY
½ oz CHERRY BRANDY
DASH OF ANGOSTURA BITTERS
1 TSP SUPERFINE SUGAR
TWIST OF LEMON PEEL
MARASCHINO CHERRY
Serve in: martini glass

Ⓨ Fill a shaker with ice.

Ⓨ Add the brandy, cherry brandy, bitters, and sugar.

Ⓨ Shake, then strain into a martini glass.

Ⓨ Decorate with the lemon twist and cherry.

Liqueurs

Liqueurs are intensely flavored, and can transform a simple cocktail into a liquid bouquet. The term "liqueur" covers a huge range of drinks, but liqueurs are essentially spirits that have been flavored and often sweetened. The flavors are derived from fruit, spices, herbs, nuts, seeds, bark, roots, and other foods.

LIQUEURS

Many liqueurs were originally tonics made by religious orders. Some of these medieval medicines are still with us: Bénédictine proclaims its monastic past in its name, and Chartreuse is made by monks to this day. The recipes for these, and many other liqueurs, still remain a secret.

Anyone who makes cocktails will have at least one bottle of liqueur in their cocktail cabinet, and often several. Fruit-based liqueurs are the most popular and versatile. Orange, for example, is the base flavor of several liqueurs, including Grand Marnier, Cointreau, and curaçao. Other fruit-based drinks include apple brandy (Calvados and applejack), cherry brandy (Kirsch), apricot brandy, melon liqueur (Midori), raspberry (crème de framboise), and banana liqueur (crème de banane).

Herb liqueurs include Galliano, which contains anise and vanilla among some 30 flavorings, and Drambuie, a Scotch-based liqueur with honey and herbs. Crème de menthe is peppermint-flavored, and comes in both green and white varieties (*see page 116*).

Then there are more exotic specimens, including Amaretto (almond), crème de cacao (cocoa), anise, and coffee liqueurs such as Tia Maria and Kahlúa. It is this huge diversity that makes the infinite variety of cocktails possible.

Golden Dawn

1 oz **CALVADOS OR APPLEJACK**
1 oz **APRICOT BRANDY**
1 oz **GIN**
1 oz **ORANGE JUICE**
SLICE OF APPLE
Serve in: Old-fashioned glass

Ψ Fill a shaker with ice.

Ψ Pour in the Calvados or applejack, apricot brandy, gin, and orange juice.

Ψ Shake.

Ψ Strain into an Old-fashioned glass.

Ψ Decorate with the apple slice.

• •

Apple Brandy Fizz

1½ oz **CALVADOS OR APPLEJACK**
1 TSP **LEMON JUICE**
GINGER ALE
SLICE OF APPLE
Serve in: highball

Ψ Shake the Calvados and lemon juice in a shaker filled with ice.

Ψ Strain into a highball half-filled with crushed ice.

Ψ Top off with the ginger ale.

Ψ Decorate with the apple slice.

Moon River

1 oz APRICOT BRANDY
1 oz COINTREAU
½ oz GALLIANO
1 oz GIN
½ oz LIME JUICE
SLICE OF LIME
Serve in: goblet

Y Fill a shaker with ice.

Y Pour in the apricot brandy, Cointreau, Galliano, and gin.

Y Add the lime juice.

Y Shake.

Y Pour into a goblet filled with ice.

Y Decorate with the lime slice.

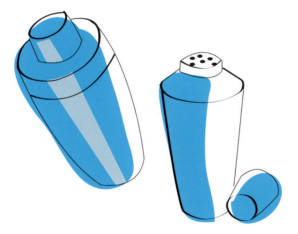

Torpedo

2 oz **SOUTHERN COMFORT**

1 oz **SCOTCH WHISKY**

Serve in: Old-fashioned glass

Y Half-fill an Old-fashioned glass with crushed ice.

Y Pour in the Southern Comfort.

Y Add the whisky, pouring it over the back of a spoon so it floats on top
of the Southern Comfort.

Valencia

1½ oz **APRICOT BRANDY**

1 oz **FRESH ORANGE JUICE**

2 DASHES **ORANGE BITTERS**

TWIST OF ORANGE PEEL

Serve in: martini glass

Y Fill a shaker with ice.

Y Add the apricot brandy, orange juice, and bitters.

Y Shake.

Y Strain into a martini glass.

Y Drop in the orange twist.

Backdraft
½ oz **DRAMBUIE**
½ oz **GRAND MARNIER**

Serve in: brandy glass, unchilled

Y Pour the Drambuie into a brandy glass.

Y Add the Grand Marnier.

Y Do not stir. Swirl the glass in your hand to release the aromas.

• •

B52
1 oz **KAHLÚA**
1 oz **BAILEY'S**
1 oz **COINTREAU**

Serve in: martini glass

Y Pour the Kahlúa into a martini glass.

Y Add the Bailey's, pouring it over
the back of a spoon so it floats on top.

Y Then add the Cointreau in the same way.

Bartender's tip
If you find it hard to get the three-layered effect, this tastes just as good lightly stirred.

Island Affair

1 oz MIDORI
½ oz COINTREAU
½ oz BLUE CURAÇAO
2 oz ORANGE JUICE
2 oz PINEAPPLE JUICE
1 oz COCONUT CREAM
WEDGE OF PINEAPPLE
MARASCHINO OR FRESH CHERRY

Serve in: highball

Ᵽ Fill a shaker with ice.

Ᵽ Add the Midori, Cointreau, blue curaçao, orange juice, pineapple juice, and coconut cream.

Ᵽ Shake well, so that the coconut cream is fully mixed in.

Ᵽ Strain into a highball.

Ᵽ Decorate with the pineapple wedge and cherry.

....

Widow's Kiss

1 oz CALVADOS OR APPLEJACK
½ oz BENEDICTINE
½ oz YELLOW CHARTREUSE
2 DASHES OF ANGOSTURA BITTERS
MARASCHINO CHERRY

Serve in: martini glass

Ᵽ Fill a shaker with ice.

Ᵽ Add the Calvados or applejack, Benedictine, Chartreuse, and bitters.

Ᵽ Shake.

Ᵽ Strain into a martini glass.

Ᵽ Drop in the cherry.

Island Affair

Fuzzy Navel

2 oz PEACH SCHNAPPS
4 oz ORANGE JUICE
SLICE OF ORANGE
Serve in: highball

Ÿ Fill a highball with ice.

Ÿ Add the Schnapps and orange juice.

Ÿ Stir.

Ÿ Decorate with the orange slice.

What's in a name?

This drink was named after the fuzz on a peach and the navel orange.

Chocolate Sundae

1 oz CRÈME DE FRAISE
¾ oz CRÈME DE CACAO
½ oz LIGHT CREAM
SMALL PIECE OF SEMISWEET CHOCOLATE, GRATED
Serve in: martini glass

Ÿ Fill a shaker with ice.

Ÿ Add the crème de fraise, crème de cacao, and cream.

Ÿ Shake well.

Ÿ Pour into a martini glass filled with crushed ice.

Ÿ Sprinkle a little grated chocolate over the top.

Incredible

½ oz **CHERRY BRANDY**
½ oz **GREEN CHARTREUSE**
1 oz **BRANDY**
MARASCHINO CHERRY
Serve in: martini glass

- Fill a mixing glass with ice.
- Add all the ingredients except the cherry.
- Stir.
- Strain into a martini glass.
- Decorate with the cherry.

Grasshopper

1 oz **CRÈME DE MENTHE**
1 oz **WHITE CRÈME DE CACAO**
1 oz **HEAVY CREAM**
Serve in: martini glass

- Fill a shaker with ice.
- Add the crème de menthe, crème de cacao, and cream.
- Shake well.
- Strain into a martini glass.

Bossa Nova

1 oz GALLIANO
1 oz WHITE RUM
½ oz APRICOT BRANDY
½ oz LEMON JUICE
1 oz PINEAPPLE JUICE
½ EGG WHITE
SLICE OF PINEAPPLE
Serve in: highball

Bartender's tip
You can leave out the egg if you prefer; the cocktail will simply be less frothy.

- ☿ Fill a shaker with ice.
- ☿ Add the Galliano, white rum, apricot brandy, lemon juice, pineapple juice, and egg white.
- ☿ Shake well, so that the egg white is fully mixed in.
- ☿ Strain into a highball.
- ☿ Decorate with the pineapple slice.

Rhett Butler

2 oz SOUTHERN COMFORT
½ oz ORANGE CURAÇAO
½ oz LEMON JUICE
½ oz LIME JUICE
1 TSP SUPERFINE SUGAR (OPTIONAL)
Serve in: cocktail glass

- ☿ Fill a shaker with ice.
- ☿ Add the Southern Comfort, curaçao, juices, and sugar, if using.
- ☿ Shake.
- ☿ Strain into a cocktail glass.

Champagne and wine

The Benedictine monk Dom Perignon is reputed to have said that champagne is like drinking stars. Among the stellar drinks in this section are the blushing Kir Royale, the bright and fizzy Mimosa, and the peachy Bellini. But it is not only sparkling wine that makes a cocktail: some great drinks are made from still white and red wine—and from fortified wines such as port, sherry, and vermouth.

CHAMPAGNE AND WINE

Champagne is the northernmost wine-making region of France. Only wine made in this relatively chilly clime can bear the name. Champagne, like other good sparkling wines, gets its fizz from being fermented twice. It has to be aged for at least one year. Vintage Champagnes, which are made from grapes harvested in the same year, are aged for much longer to round the flavor. But by no means all great Champagnes are vintage: some of the best are blends.

Sparkling wines that are made in the same way as Champagne but outside the designated region are labeled *méthode champenoise*. Cheaper fizzes are given their sparkle in vats, or are artificially carbonated. When making cocktails, you should choose a good-quality sparkler.

Consider wines from other areas of France, and from California, Spain, and Italy—you do not need to buy genuine Champagne to make a sublime cocktail. Likewise, still or table wines— both red and white wines—can be successfully used with fruit juices and other mixers.

Fortified wines also have their place in the cocktail menu. Vermouth, that essential ingredient of the Martini, the Manhattan, and many other cocktails, is probably the most versatile fortified wine, but sherry and port also make useful additions to your cocktail cabinet.

Death in the Afternoon

1 oz PERNOD
CHAMPAGNE
Serve in: champagne flute

℟ Pour the Pernod into a champagne flute.

℟ Swirl it around to coat the sides of the glass.

℟ Top off with Champagne.

Champagne Truffle

1 oz CRÈME DE CACAO
1 oz LEMON JUICE
1 TSP SUPERFINE SUGAR
3 oz CHAMPAGNE
Serve in: Old-fashioned glass

℟ Fill a shaker with ice.

℟ Add the crème de cacao, lemon juice, and sugar.

℟ Shake well.

℟ Strain into an Old-fashioned glass.

℟ Pour in the Champagne.

Bellini

1 oz PEACH SCHNAPPS
ITALIAN SPARKLING WINE
  (SUCH AS PROSECCO)
Serve in: champagne flute

℟ Pour the Peach Schnapps
  into a champagne flute.

℟ Top off with the sparkling wine.

Did you know?

This famous peach-pink cocktail was invented at Harry's Bar in Venice in 1948. It was named in honor of the 15th-century painter Giovanni Bellini, who used beautiful pinks in his paintings. The original recipe uses fresh peach purée rather than Schnapps.

Crazy Horse

1 oz **SCOTCH WHISKY**
½ oz **CRÈME DE FRAISE**
½ oz **CRÈME DE BANANE**
CHAMPAGNE

Serve in: champagne flute

Y Pour the Scotch, crème de fraise, and crème de banane into a shaker filled with ice.

Y Shake.

Y Strain into a champagne flute.

Y Top off with Champagne.

• •

Mimosa

2 oz **ORANGE JUICE**
CHAMPAGNE

Serve in: champagne flute

Y Pour the juice into a flute.

Y Top off with Champagne.

Y Stir lightly.

Did you know?

In America this refreshing pick-me-up is called a Mimosa, and in England it's called a Buck's Fizz.

• •

Grand Mimosa

2 oz **ORANGE JUICE**
1 oz **GRAND MARNIER**
CHAMPAGNE

Serve in: champagne flute

Y Pour the orange juice and Grand Marnier into a champagne flute.

Y Stir.

Y Top off with Champagne.

Y Stir lightly.

Kir Royale
¾ oz **CRÈME DE CASSIS**
CHAMPAGNE
Serve in: champagne flute

Bartender's tip
A Kir is made with dry white wine; using Champagne makes it a Kir Royale.

Ϋ Pour the crème de cassis into a
   champagne flute.
Ϋ Top off with Champagne and stir lightly.

Kir Imperiale
¾ oz **CRÈME DE FRAMBOISE**
CHAMPAGNE
Serve in: champagne flute

Ϋ Pour the crème de framboise into a champagne flute.
Ϋ Top off with Champagne.
Ϋ Stir lightly.

French 75
¼ oz **COINTREAU**
¼ oz **GIN**
½ oz **LEMON JUICE**
CHAMPAGNE
Serve in: champagne flute

Ϋ Fill a shaker with ice.
Ϋ Add the Cointreau, gin, and lemon juice.
Ϋ Shake.
Ϋ Strain into a champagne flute.
Ϋ Top off with Champagne.

Did you know?
Champagne is categorized according to its degree of dryness: brut is the driest, followed by extra sec, sec, demi-sec, and doux (sweet).

Black Velvet
GUINNESS OR OTHER STOUT
CHAMPAGNE
Serve in: highball

Ⓨ Half-fill a highball with Guinness; pour it slowly.

Ⓨ Wait for the Guinness to settle.

Ⓨ Top off with Champagne.

Did you know?
This unusual cocktail was created in 1861 to commemorate the death of Queen Victoria's beloved husband Prince Albert.

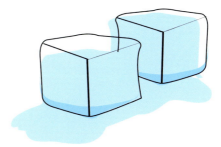

Ritz Fizz

½ oz **BLUE CURAÇAO**
½ oz **AMARETTO**
½ oz **LEMON JUICE**
CHAMPAGNE

Serve in: champagne flute

Ŷ Pour the curaçao, Amaretto, and lemon juice into a champagne flute.

Ŷ Stir.

Ŷ Top off with Champagne.

Ŷ Stir lightly.

Harry's Pick-Me-Up

1 oz **BRANDY**
1 oz **LEMON JUICE**
1 TSP **GRENADINE**
CHAMPAGNE

Serve in: champagne flute

Ŷ Fill a shaker with ice.

Ŷ Add the brandy, lemon juice, and grenadine.

Ŷ Shake, then strain into a champagne flute.

Ŷ Top off with Champagne.

Spritzer

WHITE WINE
CLUB SODA
TWIST OF LEMON PEEL

Serve in: wine glass

Ŷ Half-fill a wine glass with white wine.

Ŷ Top off with club soda.

Ŷ Drop in the lemon twist.

Ritz Fizz

Summer Red

1 TSP SUPERFINE SUGAR
1 TSP LEMON JUICE
4 oz RED WINE
CLUB SODA
TWIST OF LEMON PEEL

Serve in: wine glass

Ⴓ Put the sugar in a wine glass.

Ⴓ Add the lemon juice and stir to dissolve the sugar.

Ⴓ Pour in the red wine.

Ⴓ Top off with club soda.

Ⴓ Drop in the lemon twist.

Bartender's tip
Choose a fruity red wine such as a Merlot or a Cabernet Sauvignon for this cocktail.

• •

Sherry Cocktail

3 oz EXTRA DRY SHERRY
1 oz DRY VERMOUTH
¼ TSP LEMON JUICE
TWIST OF LEMON PEEL

Serve in: martini glass

Ⴓ Fill a shaker with ice.

Ⴓ Add the sherry, vermouth, and lemon juice.

Ⴓ Shake.

Ⴓ Strain into a martini glass.

Ⴓ Drop in the lemon twist.

Port Cocktail

3 oz PORT
1 oz WHITE CURAÇAO
2 DROPS OF ANGOSTURA BITTERS
Serve in: martini glass

Ỿ Fill a shaker with ice.

Ỿ Add the port, curaçao, and bitters.

Ỿ Shake.

Ỿ Strain into a martini glass.

Bartender's tip
A beautifully warming cocktail for cold fall evenings.

Bitter-Sweet

1 oz SWEET VERMOUTH
1 oz DRY VERMOUTH
2 DASHES ORANGE OR
  ANGOSTURA BITTERS
TWIST OF LEMON PEEL
Serve in: martini glass

Y Fill a mixing glass with ice.

Y Pour in the sweet and dry vermouths.

Y Add the bitters.

Y Stir well.

Y Strain into a martini glass.

Y Decorate with the lemon twist.

Did you know?

Vermouth is an essential ingredient of many classic cocktails including the Martini and the Manhattan. Here it is served straight, with just a dash of bitters to bring out the flavor.

Americano

2 oz SWEET VERMOUTH
1 oz CAMPARI
CLUB SODA
TWIST OF ORANGE PEEL
Serve in: Old-fashioned glass

Y Fill an Old-fashioned glass with ice.

Y Pour in the vermouth and Campari.

Y Stir.

Y Top off with club soda.

Y Decorate with the orange twist.

Did you know?

The Americano is a classic recipe that gave rise to the Negroni (*see page 78*).

Nonalcoholic

Every mixologist should have a few
nonalcoholic concoctions in the
repertoire: thirst-quenchers for hot days,
interesting combinations for drivers and
nondrinkers, or simply a refreshing
change from intoxicating drinks.
A nonalcoholic cocktail has to have
personality—it should taste so good
that the drinker doesn't notice the
absence of alcohol.

NONALCOHOLIC

To some people a nonalcoholic cocktail is a contradiction in terms, but bartenders have always offered alcohol-free versions of classics such as the Piña Colada, the Bloody Mary, and many others. And there are plenty of refreshing concoctions to which alcohol is an unnecessary and unwelcome addition: energy-boosting smoothies, for example, as well as refreshing coolers and vitamin-packed juices.

In the best tradition of cocktails, good nonalcoholic concoctions contrast flavors, such as sweetness and sharpness, in the glass. Sometimes you can get this effect simply by mixing two drinks—orange juice with bitter lemon or tonic water, for example. But a greater range of ingredients makes for a more complex drink with greater depth of flavor.

Fruit juice is the base ingredient in many nonalcoholic cocktails. You can use almost any soft fruit—blueberries, strawberries, melon, raspberries—as well as vegetables such as carrot. Grapefruit or cranberry juice will bring a welcome tartness to many sweet juice combinations, and freshly squeezed lemon or lime juice adds a zippy tang to the drink.

Sparkling apple juice or ginger ale can be used in place of the wine in Champagne cocktails to make some interesting drinks, and club soda adds length to many juice-based mixtures. Gingerroot, vanilla extract, crushed mint leaves, grenadine, or orgeat (almond) syrup all add a layer of complexity, but the strictly teetotal should steer clear of Angostura or other bitters, which contain some alcohol.

St Clement's

4 oz ORANGE JUICE
1 oz LEMON JUICE
1 TBSP SUGAR SYRUP
   (SEE PAGE 19)
CLUB SODA
SLICE OF ORANGE
SLICE OF LEMON
Serve in: highball

℧ Fill a shaker with ice.

℧ Add the orange juice, lemon juice, and sugar syrup.

℧ Shake, then strain into a highball filled with ice.

℧ Top off with club soda.

℧ Stir lightly.

℧ Decorate with the orange and lemon slices.

What's in a name?

"Oranges and lemons say the bells of St Clement's." There are two churches called St Clement's in London. Both are near the wharves where citrus fruits were once unloaded. Use freshly squeezed fruit juice for this cocktail if you can.

Free Breeze

3 oz CRANBERRY JUICE
3 oz PINEAPPLE JUICE
WEDGE OF PINEAPPLE
SPRIG OF MINT
Serve in: highball

℥ Fill a shaker with ice.

℥ Add the cranberry and pineapple juice.

℥ Shake.

℥ Strain into a highball filled with crushed ice.

℥ Decorate with the pineapple wedge and mint sprig.

• •

San Francisco

2 oz ORANGE JUICE
2 oz PINEAPPLE JUICE
2 oz GRAPEFRUIT JUICE
½ oz LEMON JUICE
1 TBSP SUGAR SYRUP (SEE PAGE 19)
DASH OF GRENADINE
CLUB SODA
SLICE OF GRAPEFRUIT
SLICE OF ORANGE
SLICE OF PINEAPPLE
Serve in: highball

℥ Fill a shaker with ice.

℥ Add the juices, sugar syrup, and grenadine.

℥ Shake.

℥ Strain into a highball filled with ice.

℥ Top off with club soda.

℥ Stir lightly.

℥ Decorate with the fruit slices.

Carmen Miranda

1 CUP CRUSHED ICE
4 oz STRAWBERRIES
½ BANANA
3 oz PLAIN YOGURT
3 oz MILK
1 TSP HONEY
DROP OF VANILLA EXTRACT
Serve in: highball

What's in a name?
Named after the 1940s Brazilian actress who was famed for her fruit-laden headwear.

℺ Put the crushed ice into a blender.

℺ Add the strawberries, reserving one for the decoration.

℺ Add the banana, yogurt, milk, honey, and vanilla extract.

℺ Blend until mixed.

℺ Pour into a highball (do not strain).

℺ Decorate with the reserved strawberry.

Virgin Mary

6 oz TOMATO JUICE
½ oz LEMON JUICE
2 DASHES WORCESTERSHIRE SAUCE
2–3 DROPS OF TABASCO
PINCH OF CELERY SALT
BLACK PEPPER
STALK OF CELERY
TWIST OF LEMON OR LIME
Serve in: highball

℺ Fill a shaker with ice.

℺ Pour in the tomato juice, lemon juice, and Worcestershire sauce.

℺ Add the Tabasco, celery salt, and a couple of grindings of black pepper.

℺ Strain into a highball filled with ice.

℺ Decorate with the celery stalk and lemon or lime twist.

Carmen Miranda

Shirley Temple

1 oz GRENADINE
GINGER ALE
WEDGE OF LEMON
2 MARASCHINO CHERRIES
Serve in: highball

℡ Pour the grenadine into a highball filled with ice.

℡ Top off with the ginger ale.

℡ Squeeze the lemon over the drink.

℡ Decorate with the cherries.

Careful Driver

ORANGE JUICE
TONIC WATER
SLICE OF ORANGE
Serve in: highball

℡ Fill a highball with ice.

℡ Half-fill with orange juice.

℡ Top off with tonic water.

℡ Decorate with the orange slice.

Did you know?

Like a Screwdriver—but this one brings no risk of penalty points on your license.

Virgin Bellini

2 oz PEACH JUICE
½ oz LEMON JUICE
1 TSP GRENADINE
CLUB SODA
Serve in: champagne flute

℡ Pour the peach juice and lemon juice into a champagne flute.

℡ Add the grenadine.

℡ Stir.

℡ Top off with club soda.

℡ Stir lightly.

On the Grape Vine

2½ oz WHITE GRAPE JUICE
1 oz LEMON JUICE
DASH OF GRENADINE
Serve in: martini glass

Y Fill a shaker with ice.

Y Add the grape juice, lemon juice, and grenadine.

Y Shake, then strain into a martini glass.

Apple Fizz

2 oz APPLE JUICE
DASH OF GRENADINE
GINGER BEER OR ALE
Serve in: highball

Y Fill a highball with ice.

Y Pour in the apple juice.

Y Add the grenadine and stir.

Y Top off with the ginger beer or ale.

Y Stir lightly.

Nada Colada

3 oz PINEAPPLE JUICE
1½ oz COCONUT CREAM
MARASCHINO CHERRY
Serve in: martini glass

Y Fill a shaker with ice.

Y Add the pineapple juice and coconut cream.

Y Shake, then strain into a martini glass.

Y Decorate with the cherry.

GLOSSARY

Advocaat Dutch liqueur made with egg yolks, sugar, and brandy.

Amaretto almond liqueur from Italy.

Anejo tequila tequila that has been aged for several years (*anejo* is the Spanish word for old); you can also get *anejo* rum.

Angostura bitters alcoholic bitter tonic used as a flavoring in mixed drinks and cocktails.

Anise liqueur flavored with aniseed. Anisette is similar, but sweeter.

Aperitif drink taken before dinner, to stimulate the appetite.

Apple brandy brandy made from fermented apples. The best-known type is Calvados which is made in Normandy, France; Applejack is made in the United States.

Applejack American apple brandy.

Apricot brandy brandy made from fermented apricots.

Apricot liqueur liqueur flavored with apricots.

Armagnac brandy distilled from wine and made in a designated region of southwest France.

Bacardi the best-known brand of white rum.

Bailey's a blend of Irish whiskey, cream, and chocolate.

Benedictine sweet liqueur flavored with a secret blend of herbs and medicinal plants.

Bitters bitter or bitter-sweet flavoring made from herbs, plant extracts, and spices. Angostura is the best-known brand.

Blended Scotch whisky combination of grain whisky and single malts: up to 40 different malts may be used in a blended Scotch.

Blue curaçao orange-flavored liqueur with blue coloring.

Bourbon American whiskey distilled from a grain mash of at least 51 percent corn plus barley, rye, and wheat. It is aged in charred oak casks.

Brandy spirit distilled from fermented fruit. True brandy is made from grapes, and includes Cognac and Armagnac; fruit brandies include apricot, cherry, and apple.

Cachaca Brazilian sugarcane spirit similar to rum.

Calvados apple brandy made in Normandy, France.

Campari Italian orange bitters with a bright red appearance used as a flavoring or served as an aperitif.

Canadian whisky blended whisky made in Canada.

Chambord brand of black raspberry liqueur.

Champagne sparkling wine produced in the Champagne region of France.

Chartreuse liqueur containing more than 130 herbs and spices made by Carthusian monks near Grenoble, France. There is green and yellow Chartreuse; the green is heavier with a higher proof. Chartreuse can be served as a digestif or used as a flavoring.

Chaser short drink taken after a shot of spirit.

Cocktail onions tiny picked onions that are used (rinsed) as a decoration for a Gibson.

Coconut liqueur sweet coconut-flavored liqueur which is based on rum.

Coconut rum flavoured rum. Malibu is the best-known brand.

Cognac fine French brandy.

Cointreau clear liqueur flavored with the rind of bitter oranges. Cointreau is a triple sec, which is another term for white curaçao.

Cream liqueur a cream liqueur is spirit-based and contains cream. Bailey's Irish Cream is the best-known brand.

Crème de banane banana liqueur.

Crème de cacao cocoa-flavored liqueur.

Crème de café coffee liqueur.

Crème de cassis black currant liqueur.

Crème de coconut coconut liqueur.

Crème de framboise raspberry liqueur.

Crème de menthe peppermint liqueur, available in green or white (colorless).

Crème de mûre blackberry liqueur.

Crème de noyaux almond liqueur. It can be pink or white (colorless).

Curaçao liqueur flavored with orange rind. Curacao can be white (called triple sec), blue, orange, or other colors—but the flavor is always orange.

Dark rum rum that has been aged in casks for a long period, though sometimes the color comes from the addition of caramel.

Digestif drink taken after dinner to aid the digestion.

Drambuie Scottish liqueur based on whisky and flavored with herbs and honey.

Dutch gin type of gin, also known as genever.

Fortified wine wine strengthened with another form of alcohol, usually a neutral-tasting spirit. Port, sherry, vermouth, and madeira are all fortified wines.

Framboise French for raspberry; the word is often used to denote raspberry liqueur.

Frangelico Italian hazelnut liqueur.

French vermouth vermouth produced in France. It is drier than Italian vermouth.

Galliano Italian herb flavored with over 40 herbs, flowers, and spices, including aniseed, vanilla and honey.

Gold rum rum that has been aged for several years, though sometimes the color is due to the addition of caramel.

Gomme syrup sugar syrup.

Grand Marnier orange-flavored liqueur which has Cognac as its base spirit.

Grappa Italian spirit made from the pressed skins and seeds of grapes, usually served as a digestif.

Grenadine a strong, blood-red syrup made from pomegranates. It is used as sweetener and contains no alcohol.

Jamaica rum dark rum made in Jamaica from molasses.

Kahlúa coffee liqueur from Mexico.

Kirsch fruit brandy made from black cherries.

Kümmel liqueur flavored with caraway seeds.

Light rum rum aged for less than a year; it is also called white rum as it is colorless. Bacardi is the best-known brand.

Lime cordial concentrated lime juice; Rose's is a well-known brand.

Liqueur spirit that been distilled or mixed with a flavoring.

Liquor American term for an alcoholic drink.

London Dry gin the clear, dry gin used in cocktails and mixed drinks. Its name refers to the fact that it was first made in London.

Madeira fortified wine aged in casks; it is made on the island of Madeira.

Mandarine Napoléon Belgian tangerine-flavored liqueur, based on brandy.

Maraschino cherry decoration for cocktails. The cherries come in jars of cherry-flavored liqueur, which is used as an ingredient in some cocktails.

Mescal Mexican spirit made from the agave plant. It is similar to tequila, but of lesser quality.

Midori Japanese bright green liqueur made from melon.

Molasses brown syrup that is produced as a by-product of sugar refining; it can be turned into rum.

Orange bitters bitters made from the peel of sour oranges.

Orgeat syrup almond-flavored syrup used as a sweetener.

Pastis French liqueur made with aniseed or licorice. The most infamously strong pastis is absinthe, which is illegal in many countries.

Pernod spirit flavored with star anise, giving it a licorice flavor.

Peychaud's bitters brand of bitters produced in the United States.

Pimm's English liqueur made from gin, fruits, herbs, and spices. Usually served with lemonade or ginger ale.

Pisco clear South American brandy made from the Muscat grape.

Plymouth gin clear gin similar to London Dry, but drier. It is made by one company in the English naval town of Plymouth.

Poire William pear liqueur.

Port fortified wine from Portugal. It can be white, ruby or tawny.

Sambuca anise-flavored Italian liqueur made by infusing licorice and extract of elder.

Schnapps originally a Scandinavian spirit made from grain or potato; now used as a name for fruit liqueurs including peach, apple, cinnamon and other flavors.

Slivovitz plum brandy.

Sloe gin liqueur made by steeping sloe berries in gin.

Sour mix a combination of lemon and lime juice sweetened with sugar.

Southern Comfort bourbon-based liqueur flavored with peach.

Strega Italian liqueur flavored with spices and herbs including mint, fennel, and saffron.

Sugar syrup sweetener often used in cocktails. It is commercially available (often called gomme syrup) but you can easily make your own (see page 19).

Tabasco hot pepper-flavored sauce used as a flavoring.

Triple sec liqueur flavored with sweet and bitter orange peel. The best-known brand is Cointreau; another, Grand Marnier, is similar. Triple sec is a white (colorless) curaçao.

Tuaca Italian citrus liqueur.

Van den Hum tangerine-flavored liqueur from South Africa.

Vermouth fortified wine infused with herbs, sugar and caramel. You can get dry or sweet vermouth; sweet vermouth can be red or white.

Worcestershire sauce spicy sauce used as a flavoring.

WEBSITES

There are many cocktail websites which allow you to search for recipes that contain a specific ingredient. So if you have a bottle of, say, Southern Comfort or crème de framboise, you can find ideas for different ways of using it. Some websites also allow you to search for cocktails of a particular color, or for long or short drinks, aperitifs, digestifs, and so on.

www.bolscocktail.com

www.webtender.com

www.drinkalizer.com

www.drinkmixer.com

www.barnonedrinks.com

INDEX

ACKNOWLEDGMENTS

The author and publishers are grateful to the owners of KOBA, and to Dre Hucko, mixologist, for their assistance in preparing the cocktails photographed in this book.

KOBA
135 Western Road
Brighton BN1 2LA
U.K.
tel: (+44) 1273 720059
www.kobauk.com